Holy Glow-Up:
365 Days to Shine from Within

A Year of Faith, Healing, and Radiant Renewal

Kelley McConnell

Crossroad to Healing Publishing

Holy Glow-Up:
365 Days to Shine from Within

© 2025 Kelley McConnell

All rights reserved. No part of this book may be reproduced or transmitted in any form or by any means electronic, mechanical, photocopying, recording, or otherwise without prior written permission from the author, except for brief quotations in reviews or articles.

Scripture quotations taken from the Holy Bible, New International Version® NIV®.

Copyright © 1973, 1978, 1984, 2011 by Biblica, Inc.TM Used by permission. All rights reserved worldwide.

Published by Crossroad to Healing Publishing

For inquiries or permissions: crossroadtohealing@gmail.com

Printed in the United States of America
ISBN: 979-8-9938822-0-8

Acknowledgments

To everyone who believed in this vision from the very beginning, thank you.

To my *Crossroad to Healing* community, for your faith, encouragement, and testimonies that continue to inspire my purpose. You've shown me that healing happens in sacred community: one prayer, one breakthrough, one Glow-Up at a time.

To my family and friends, for your love, patience, and endless grace as this book took form page by page.

To every woman who reminded me that our stories matter, your strength and surrender helped shape this devotional more than you'll ever know.

And above all, to God, the Author of restoration and the source of every Holy Glow-Up. Every word in these pages belongs to Him.

A Gift of Light

To your Shining Light: _____

With Radiant Love From:_____

On this Day of your Glow:_____

This glow is meant to be shared, one heart, one day, one light at a time.

May your heart forever shine in His light.

Dedication

For the hearts who lit the path beside me and inspired me through and through.

To my parents,
Who gave me the firm foundation and rooted me in Christ. Though I sometimes drifted, it was that same foundation that led me back to the cross: back to grace, to healing, and to Him.

To my family,
Especially my husband, John, who has faithfully supported every wild idea, stood by me through every storm, and believed in my calling even when the path seemed uncertain.

And to my children,
You inspire me to love more fully, seek truth more deeply, and live each day as a reflection of Christ's light and love. Your joy and strength remind me daily why God placed this mission on my heart.

To my sister, Tracey,
Who helped bring me back to Christ through music when my spirit was weary and my heart was heavy. Your encouragement during one of my hardest seasons reminded me that music is ministry, a way for the soul to pray when words fall short. You helped me rediscover my voice, not just in song but in faith, and for that I will always thank God for you.

To my dear friends and sisters in Christ:
Alyssa, Eleni and the many others God has woven into my journey. Your faith, encouragement, and shared prayers have been divine reminders that God never calls us to walk alone. Each of you has carried a piece of this journey through your love, light, and unwavering belief.

To Lisa,
Your daily devotionals, steadfast faith, and loving reminders to stay anchored in God's Word reignited my own light. Your consistency in Christ has been a spark in this vision: proof that small, faithful acts can transform hearts and lives. Your sisterhood has been a wellspring of grace and divine timing, this book truly carries your imprint.

To Nicole,
Your courage, grace, and unwavering faith have inspired me beyond words. Your gentle wisdom and Spirit-led insight have brought divine clarity and peace to this journey, living proof that when we invite God into our work, He breathes life into every word.

And to your precious son, Wesley, whose light continues to shine so brightly, thank you for reminding me that Heaven is not far away, and that love never ends. Your story and his spirit have been sacred mirrors of faith, hope, and eternal connection, leaving an indelible mark on my own walk with God.

To my Crossroad to Healing community,
Every soul who has walked through my doors or shared a part of their story: you've shown me the divine beauty of resilience, grace, and restoration.

And to every woman who has ever felt dimmed by life's storms,

This is your holy reminder that your glow never left, it was simply waiting to rise again.

You are rooted in love, guided in faith, and destined to shine.

With all my heart,
Kelley

For Aubrey
The Light That Shines Ahead

My sweet girl,

You are the living reflection of everything this book was meant to be: faith in motion, grace in bloom, and light that never fades.

Watching you grow into the young woman God created you to be fills my heart with awe and gratitude.

May you always walk with confidence, speak with kindness, and let your faith shine brighter than any fear.

You don't have to search for your glow, my love, it's already within you.

Keep shining boldly. Keep loving deeply. Keep walking with Jesus every step of the way.
You are my greatest glow.

Mom

"You are the light of the world. A city set on a hill cannot be hidden."
Matthew 5:14

A Prayer of Dedication

Heavenly Father,

May every word in these pages draw hearts closer to You.

Let this devotional become a vessel of healing, renewal, and radiant faith for every soul who opens it.

Bless each reader with peace that surpasses understanding and joy that overflows from Your Spirit.

May Your light shine through every reflection, every affirmation, and every moment of surrender.

In Jesus' Name, Amen.

"Every good and perfect gift is from above."
James 1:17

Introduction
Welcome to Your Holy Glow-Up

A 365-Day Journey to Restore Your Faith, Renew Your Peace, and Reclaim Your Glow

You were never meant to dim your light just to fit in.
You were created to glow from within.

This isn't a glow that fades with trends or seasons. It's the kind that's born through faith, refined by grace, and sustained by the presence of God.

A Holy Glow-Up isn't about outer perfection. It's about inner transformation: the kind that happens when you root yourself in Christ, surrender what no longer serves you, and allow His Spirit to illuminate every corner of your being.

Each day of this devotional is designed to help you realign your heart, renew your mind, and restore your spirit. Each phase of your Holy Glow-Up unfolds at its own pace. Some are brief and reflective, others full and radiant, just as every season of faith moves uniquely in God's timing.

You'll find short readings, affirmations to speak life over yourself, and Glow-Up Challenges to help you live your faith out loud. Let this book be your mirror of divine reflection, reminding you who you are and whose you are.

You are radiant. You are restored. You are rooted in grace and glowing with purpose.

Here's to 365 days of shining from within: through faith, through healing, through every season.

Your Holy Glow-Up begins now.

How to Use This Book

There's no wrong way to begin your Holy Glow-Up. You can start on any date, return to favorite days, or linger in a phase that speaks deeply to your heart. Each day offers a rhythm of:

Scripture ✦ *Reflection* ✦ *Affirmation* ✦ *Glow-Up Challenge*

Pause when prompted, pray when moved,

and let God guide the pace.

This journey isn't about perfection. It's about presence.

Table of Phases & Structure

A woman of faith doesn't just find her light, she grows through it.

Phase 1: Rooted in Christ ✧ Establishing your foundation of faith.
Theme: Faith, identity, surrender, and spiritual grounding. Days 1-73

Phase 2: Healed from Within ✧ Allowing God to restore what was once broken.
Theme: Healing, restoration, forgiveness, and inner peace. Days 74-120

Phase 3: Glow Through the Storm ✧ Finding light even when skies turn gray.
Theme: Endurance, trust, and divine strength. Days 121–169

Phase 4: Radiant Faith ✧ Living boldly in your calling and reflecting His light.
Theme: Purpose, faith in action, gratitude, and bold belief. Days 170–218

Phase 5: Restored to Shine ✧ Embodying wholeness, balance, and radiant peace.
Theme: Renewal, alignment, purpose, and spiritual fullness. Days 219–365

Reflection & Renewal

At the end of each phase, you'll find short moments for reflection and journaling. These are gentle invitations to pause, breathe, and thank God for how far you've come.

Your Glow-Up Flow

Scripture ✦ Reflection ✦ Affirmation ✦ Glow-Up Challenge

Welcome to Your Holy Glow-Up

You were never meant to dim, only to shine through Him.

Dear Beautiful Soul,

If you've picked up this book, you're already saying "yes" to something divine. You're saying yes to healing. Yes to faith. Yes to a deeper glow: one that doesn't fade with time or circumstance, because it flows from the Light within you.

The world teaches us to chase after radiance to earn love, approval, or worth. But true glow doesn't come from the surface. It's born in the sacred space where your spirit meets His Spirit... where roots run deep, storms refine, and healing becomes holy.

Over the next 365 days, you'll walk through five sacred phases, each designed to help you rediscover your inner light and strengthen your walk with Christ.

Rooted in Christ: building your foundation in faith.

Healed from Within: allowing God to restore what the world tried to break.

Glow Through the Storm: finding peace and power even in pain.

Radiant Faith: stepping boldly into purpose with unshakable confidence.

Restored to Shine: living in alignment, balance, and divine joy.

Each Day Offers a Simple Rhythm to Keep Your Heart Aligned:

Scripture ✦ *Reflection* ✦ *Affirmation* ✦ *Glow-Up Challenge*

You don't have to be perfect to glow, you just have to be willing. Let this be your daily invitation to pause, breathe, and let God's light do what only He can do: restore, renew, and radiate through you.

As you journey through these pages, may you remember your glow flows from grace.

It's about surrendering. It's about letting God's love move through every part of your life until what was once broken begins to shine again.

This is your season to rise, reflect, and radiate.

Your Holy Glow-Up begins now.

With love and light,

Kelley

Phase 1
Rooted in Christ

Before you can rise, you must be rooted.

This first phase of your Holy Glow-Up is about returning to your foundation: the deep, steady connection between you and God. When you're rooted in His truth, no storm can shake you, no season can strip you of your purpose.

Being rooted means trusting the unseen work beneath the surface. It's learning to rest in His timing, even when growth feels slow. It's choosing to build your life on faith rather than fear, peace rather than perfection.

In this phase, let God pull you closer to His presence.
Let Him nourish the soil of your soul with grace, peace, and truth. Because once your roots are deep in Him, your glow will be unshakable, steady, strong, and holy.

Rooted in Christ

Day 1
Planted on Purpose

January 1

"They are like trees planted along a riverbank, with roots that reach deep into the water."
Jeremiah 17:8

Every season of your life, including the dry ones, the stormy ones, and the waiting ones is nourishing your roots. God doesn't waste a drop of what you've walked through. You're planted, not buried.

Affirmation: I am rooted in God's truth and nourished by His living water.

Glow-Up Challenge: Step outside today and thank God for where He's planted you even if it doesn't look perfect yet.

Rooted in Christ

Day 2
Faith Before Feelings

January 2

"For we live by faith, not by sight."
2 Corinthians 5:7

Some days faith feels quiet, like a whisper under the noise of worry. But your spirit knows: even when nothing looks like it's working, God is still moving.

Affirmation: My faith is stronger than my fear.

Glow-Up Challenge: When doubt shows up, speak faith out loud. Say, "God is working this out for my good."

Rooted in Christ

Day 3
Peace Over Perfection

January 3

"Then you will experience God's peace, which exceeds anything we can understand."
Philippians 4:7

You don't have to have it all together to be held by His peace. God meets you in the mess, not after it's cleaned up.

Affirmation: I release control and receive peace that passes understanding.

Glow-Up Challenge: Breathe deeply for one minute, thanking God for His peace in this exact moment.

Rooted in Christ

Day 4
Your Worth Is Rooted

January 4

"I praise You because I am fearfully and wonderfully made."
Psalm 139:14

Your worth isn't in your productivity, your reflection, or your past. It's anchored in the image of God Himself.

Affirmation: My identity is rooted in divine worth, unshakable, undeniable, unearned.

Glow-Up Challenge: Look in the mirror and speak one truth you love about the woman God created you to be.

Rooted in Christ

Day 5
Let God Prune

January 5

"He cuts off every branch that bears no fruit... while every branch that does bear fruit He prunes so that it will be even more fruitful."
John 15:2

Sometimes what feels like loss is really preparation for abundance. God's pruning is proof of His care.

Affirmation: I trust God's pruning process. He is shaping me for greater fruitfulness.

Glow-Up Challenge: Release one thing today that no longer aligns with your peace or purpose.

Rooted in Christ

Day 6
Stay Watered

January 6

"The Lord will guide you continually, giving you water when you are dry."
Isaiah 58:11

You can't pour from an empty cup, and even Jesus rested. Refresh your soul with stillness, Scripture, and presence.

Affirmation: I stay connected to the Source that never runs dry.

Glow-Up Challenge: Drink an extra glass of water today and whisper, "Lord, refill my spirit, too."

Rooted in Christ

Day 7
Rooted & Radiant

January 7

"Let your roots grow down into Him, and let your lives be built on Him."
Colossians 2:7

When your foundation is faith, your glow doesn't fade; it deepens. You shine differently when your roots are holy.

Affirmation: My glow comes from being rooted in Christ: steady, strong, and radiant.

Glow-Up Challenge: Light a candle or turn on soft worship music tonight as a reminder that your light is meant to be seen.

Rooted in Christ

Day 8
Grow Where God Guides

January 8

"Seek His will in all you do, and He will show you which path to take."
Proverbs 3:6

You don't have to have it all figured out, you just have to keep walking with Him. God doesn't always hand out maps. Sometimes He gives you just enough light for the next step. Trust that where He leads, growth will follow.

Affirmation: I am guided by divine direction. Every step I take is lit by His wisdom.

Glow-Up Challenge: Say a prayer before you make your next big or small decision. Ask, "Lord, align my steps with Yours."

Rooted in Christ

Day 9
Root Before You Bloom

January 9

"To everything there is a season, a time for every purpose under heaven."
Ecclesiastes 3:1

The world celebrates blooms, but God celebrates roots. Growth that lasts begins underground, where no one sees. Don't rush your process. Your bloom will come right on time.

Affirmation: My roots are growing strong beneath the surface. My season to bloom is unfolding perfectly.

Glow-Up Challenge: Reflect on one area of your life that's still "in progress" and thank God for the unseen growth.

Rooted in Christ

Day 10
Stay Anchored in Peace

January 10

"Let the peace of Christ rule in your hearts."
Colossians 3:15

Peace isn't the absence of problems. It's the presence of Jesus in the middle of them. Let His peace be your anchor when emotions try to toss you around.

Affirmation: My heart is anchored in peace that only Christ provides.

Glow-Up Challenge: When something stressful arises today, pause and whisper, "Jesus, center me in Your peace."

Rooted in Christ

Day 11
Faith Has Roots Too

January 11

"Faith is the substance of things hoped for, the evidence of things not seen."
Hebrews 11:1

Faith doesn't need proof to believe. It just needs roots deep enough to trust. Keep watering your faith with prayer and truth, even when you can't yet see the fruit.

Affirmation: My faith is deeply rooted. I trust what I cannot yet see.

Glow-Up Challenge: Write down one prayer you've been waiting on and add, "I trust Your timing, Lord."

Rooted in Christ

Day 12
Nourish Your Soul Daily

January 12

"People do not live by bread alone, but by every word that comes from the mouth of God."
Matthew 4:4

You feed your body every day. Your soul deserves the same care. Let Scripture, prayer, and worship refill what the world drains.

Affirmation: I nourish my soul with truth, presence, and the Word of God.

Glow-Up Challenge: Spend 10 quiet minutes in Scripture or worship before scrolling or starting your day.

Rooted in Christ

Day 13
Rest Is Holy

January 13

"My presence will go with you, and I will give you rest."
Exodus 33:14

Rest isn't laziness, it's faith in motion. When you slow down, you make room for God to move. True rest nourishes both body and spirit.

Affirmation: Rest is my act of faith. I release, I restore, I renew.

Glow-Up Challenge: Take one intentional pause today: no phone, no noise. Just breathe and invite His presence in.

Rooted in Christ

Day 14
Deep Roots, Steady Heart

January 14

"They are like trees planted by streams of water, which yield fruit in season."
Psalm 1:3

The deeper your roots go, the stronger your peace becomes. You don't need to fear the winds of change when you're grounded in the One who never moves.

Affirmation: My spirit stands firm: rooted in grace, steady in truth, and watered by peace.

Glow-Up Challenge: Write a note of gratitude for something that has kept you grounded through a hard season.

Rooted in Christ

Day 15
Grace Over Guilt

January 15

"So now there is no condemnation for those who belong to Christ Jesus."
Romans 8:1

You were never meant to live chained to what God has already forgiven. Grace doesn't excuse the past, it redeems it. Let go of guilt, and let His mercy rewrite your story.

Affirmation: I release guilt and receive grace. I walk free in the love of Christ.

Glow-Up Challenge: Write down one thing you've been hard on yourself about. Then cross it out and write "grace won."

Rooted in Christ

Day 16
Let Faith Do the Heavy Lifting

January 16

"Come to me, all you who are weary and burdened, and I will give you rest."
Matthew 11:28

You don't have to carry it all. Having faith allows you to put down the weight of effort in favor of holding trust. When you lay it down at His feet, He lifts what you can't.

Affirmation: I trade striving for surrender and strength for trust.

Glow-Up Challenge: Pray, "Lord, I hand this to You," and physically open your hands as you release it.

Rooted in Christ

Day 17
Faith in the Waiting

January 17

"Wait patiently for the Lord. Be brave and courageous."
Psalm 27:14

Waiting isn't wasted time, it's where faith matures. What feels like a pause is often God preparing the path ahead.

Affirmation: I am not behind; I'm being prepared.

Glow-Up Challenge: List three blessings that came after a season of waiting, and thank God for His perfect timing.

Rooted in Christ

Day 18
Roots Before Recognition

January 18

"Whoever is faithful in little things will be faithful in much."
Luke 16:10

The quiet work you do in obscurity is seen by Heaven. Faithfulness in small things is how God builds trust for greater things. You're not unnoticed. You're under development.

Affirmation: I am faithful in the small, and God is faithful in the big.

Glow-Up Challenge: Do something kind today that no one else will see, and let that be your worship.

Rooted in Christ

Day 19
Stay Connected to the Source

January 19

"I am the vine; you are the branches. If you remain in me and I in you, you will bear much fruit."
John 15:5

Your glow fades when you disconnect from the Source. Stay close through prayer, worship, and stillness, not performance. Fruit flows from connection, not effort.

Affirmation: I remain in Him, and He remains in me. Together we bear fruit that lasts.

Glow-Up Challenge: Turn off distractions and spend five minutes just being with God, no agenda, just presence.

Rooted in Christ

Day 20
Unshaken by Storms

January 20

"The rain came down, the streams rose, and the winds blew ... yet it did not fall, because it had its foundation on the rock."
Matthew 7:25

The winds will come, but so will God's strength. Being rooted doesn't mean you never bend, it means you don't break.

Affirmation: I stand firm on the Rock that never moves.

Glow-Up Challenge: Journal a time you thought you'd fall but God held you steady. That's your evidence of faith.

Rooted in Christ

Day 21
Bloom in Gratitude

January 21

"Give thanks in all circumstances; for this is God's will for you."
1 Thessalonians 5:18

Gratitude turns ordinary moments into holy ground. When you thank God in the middle of what you don't understand, you plant seeds for future blessings.

Affirmation: I am grateful for this season because it is growing me into who God designed me to be.

Glow-Up Challenge: Write down five things you're thankful for even the hard ones. Gratitude shifts your glow.

Rooted in Christ

Day 22
Divine Alignment

January 22

"We can make our plans, but the Lord determines our steps."
Proverbs 16:9

You can plan, dream, and design your path, but divine alignment always has the final say. God's direction is not always the fastest route, but it's always the most fulfilling one.

Affirmation: I trust God to realign my steps toward His best for me.

Glow-Up Challenge: Ask God today, "Redirect me where I've drifted from Your will." Then notice what peace points you back to center.

Rooted in Christ

Day 23
Guard Your Garden

January 23

"Above all else, guard your heart, for everything you do flows from it."
Proverbs 4:23

Your heart is sacred soil. Protect it from negativity, comparison, and doubt. Not everyone deserves planting rights in your garden. Keep your peace fenced with prayer.

Affirmation: My heart is guarded by grace. Only love and light take root here.

Glow-Up Challenge: Pay attention to what drains you today, and gently release it to protect your peace.

Rooted in Christ

Day 24
Bloom Without Competing

January 24

"Pay careful attention to your own work... then you will get the satisfaction of a job well done."
Galatians 6:4

Your glow doesn't dim someone else's, and theirs doesn't diminish yours. God made room for everyone's bloom. Stay focused on your lane; comparison is just distraction in disguise.

Affirmation: I bloom in my own divine timing. I am not in competition, I am in purpose.

Glow-Up Challenge: Compliment someone genuinely today. Gratitude grows faster when it's shared.

Rooted in Christ

Day 25
When Faith Feels Small

January 25

*"If you have faith as small as a mustard seed...
nothing will be impossible for you."
Matthew 17:20*

God doesn't need perfect faith, just present faith. Even the smallest seed can move mountains when planted in the right soil.

Affirmation: My faith may feel small, but my God is mighty.

Glow-Up Challenge: Whisper one small prayer today, even if all you can say is, "Lord, help me trust You."

Rooted in Christ

Day 26
Rooted in Obedience

January 26

"Do not merely listen to the word, and so deceive yourselves. Do what it says."
James 1:22

Obedience can at times feel like control, but it's actually aligning your heart to His. When you follow God's nudge, you unlock blessings your own plans could never reach.

Affirmation: I walk in obedience, even when I don't understand the outcome.

Glow-Up Challenge: Take one small action today that you've been hesitating on. Faith moves when you do.

Rooted in Christ

Day 27
Let Light In

January 27

"I am the light of the world. Whoever follows Me will never walk in darkness."
John 8:12

Light doesn't chase darkness: it replaces it. When you let Jesus' light fill your heart, fear and confusion have no room left to stay.

Affirmation: I walk in light, not in fear. My spirit glows with divine clarity.

Glow-Up Challenge: Spend a few moments in sunlight or by a window today, and let it remind you of the light that lives within you.

Rooted in Christ

Day 28
Stronger Than You Know

January 28

"But those who trust in the Lord will renew their strength."
Isaiah 40:31

When you feel weary, remember, even roots rest. Strength isn't always loud. Sometimes it's the quiet endurance to keep believing, even when it hurts, that allows God to lift the heaviest weights in our lives.

Affirmation: My strength is renewed daily through the Spirit within me.

Glow-Up Challenge: Speak this out loud three times: "I am stronger than I feel, because God is my strength."

Rooted in Christ

Day 29
Stay Consistent in the Small

January 29

"Whatever you do, work at it with all your heart, as working for the Lord, not for human masters."
Colossians 3:23

Consistency builds character. God notices every quiet prayer, every small act of faith, every time you choose peace over panic. The little things water big roots.

Affirmation: I show up faithfully in the small and trust God to multiply it.

Glow-Up Challenge: Pick one spiritual habit prayer, journaling, or worship and commit to doing it daily this week.

Rooted in Christ

Day 30
Bloom Where You're Becoming

January 30

"He who began a good work in you will carry it on to completion."
Philippians 1:6

You are not unfinished, you are unfolding. God doesn't rush beauty. He reveals it layer by layer. Be proud of your process.

Affirmation: I am a beautiful work in progress, guided by grace and growth.

Glow-Up Challenge: Write down three ways you've grown in the last year, even if they were born from hard seasons.

Rooted in Christ

Day 31
Roots of Rest

January 31

"My soul finds rest in God alone."
Psalm 62:1

Rest isn't idleness, it's intimacy. When your soul slows down, you hear Heaven more clearly. Deep rest restores your strength to keep blooming.

Affirmation: My rest is sacred. I find renewal in His presence.

Glow-Up Challenge: Schedule 15 minutes of quiet today: no phone, no background noise, just stillness with God.

Rooted in Christ

Day 32
Faith Over Feelings

February 1

"So we fix our eyes not on what is seen, but on what is unseen."
2 Corinthians 4:18

Feelings can shift like the wind, but faith is your anchor. When emotions rise, remember your roots go deeper than what you feel.

Affirmation: I am grounded in faith, not swayed by fleeting feelings.

Glow-Up Challenge: When you feel overwhelmed, say out loud, "My feelings are valid, but my faith is stronger."

Rooted in Christ

Day 33
Rooted in Gratitude

February 2

"Let your roots grow down into Him, then your faith will grow strong and you will overflow with thankfulness."
Colossians 2:7

Gratitude turns ordinary days into holy ones. Every time you say, "Thank You," you strengthen your connection to God's goodness.

Affirmation: I overflow with thankfulness. Gratitude is my glow.

Glow-Up Challenge: Write or speak five "Thank Yous": one for something big, one for something small, and three for things you often overlook.

Rooted in Christ

Day 34
When You Feel Dry

February 3

"For I will pour water on the thirsty land and streams on the dry ground."
Isaiah 44:3

Even the most rooted souls have dry seasons. Don't fear them. They are invitations to seek the Source again. God will refill what's been poured out.

⚜

Affirmation: I may feel empty, but I am never abandoned. God is refilling me now.

Glow-Up Challenge: Whisper a simple prayer today: "Lord, pour Your living water into the dry places of my heart."

Rooted in Christ

Day 35
Rooted in Joy

February 4

"The joy of the Lord is your strength."
Nehemiah 8:10

Joy isn't something you chase. It's something that grows when you're rooted in His love. It's the fruit of deep faith and divine trust.

Affirmation: My joy is unshakable because it's rooted in the Lord.

Glow-Up Challenge: Do one thing today that makes your spirit smile, dance, laugh, sing, or sit in the sun. Joy is worship too.

Rooted in Christ

Day 36
When You Don't Feel It

February 5

"Be still, and know that I am God."
Psalm 46:10

Some days, faith feels silent. The glow dims. But even when your emotions can't trace Him, your spirit still knows Him. God doesn't leave when you go quiet, He leans in closer.

Affirmation: Even in silence, God is near. My stillness makes room for His presence.

Glow-Up Challenge: Sit in complete stillness for three minutes today and repeat: "God, You are here."

Rooted in Christ

Day 37
Unshakeable Roots

February 6

"Be steadfast, immovable, always abounding in the work of the Lord."
1 Corinthians 15:58

Being rooted doesn't mean life is easy. It means you're grounded in something eternal. When the world wavers, your foundation stays firm because it's built on His Word.

Affirmation: My roots are unshakable because they're planted in God's promises.

Glow-Up Challenge: Write one Scripture that has anchored you lately and place it somewhere you'll see it daily.

Rooted in Christ

Day 38
God's Timing Is Never Late

February 7

"He has made everything beautiful in its time."
Ecclesiastes 3:11

Waiting tests the heart, but God's timing is artistry. Every delay is design. He's not making you wait to punish you. He's aligning everything perfectly for your purpose.

※

Affirmation: I trust that God's timing is never delayed; it's divine.

Glow-Up Challenge: Write down one thing you've been waiting for and instead of asking when, start thanking God for how He's preparing it.

Rooted in Christ

Day 39
Rooted in Forgiveness

February 8

"Be kind to one another, tenderhearted, forgiving one another, as God in Christ forgave you."
Ephesians 4:32

Forgiveness frees the soil of your soul. Holding onto bitterness blocks your own growth. Forgive not because they deserve it, but because you deserve peace.

Affirmation: I choose forgiveness to make room for peace and freedom.

Glow-Up Challenge: Say a silent prayer for someone who hurt you. Bless them and release them into God's hands.

Rooted in Christ

Day 40
Strength in Still Seasons

February 9

"In quietness and trust shall be your strength."
Isaiah 30:15

Stillness is not stagnation. It's strength training for your spirit. God builds your endurance in the quiet spaces where faith grows roots.

Affirmation: I find strength in stillness and power in patience.

Glow-Up Challenge: Take a walk without music or distraction today, and listen for what your heart's been trying to say.

Rooted in Christ

Day 41
Nourished by the Word

February 10

"Your word is a lamp to my feet and a light to my path."
Psalm 119:105

Scripture is spiritual nourishment. Every verse you read, every word you meditate on, feeds the roots of your faith and helps you grow steady in truth.

Affirmation: God's Word nourishes me daily. I walk in its light and wisdom.

Glow-Up Challenge: Choose one verse today to memorize, let it speak life over your next 24 hours.

Rooted in Christ

Day 42
The Glow of Gratitude

February 11

"Give thanks to the Lord, for He is good; His love endures forever."
1 Chronicles 16:34

Gratitude keeps your glow steady. It reminds your heart of how far God has already brought you. The more you thank Him, the more you'll see His fingerprints in your story.

Affirmation: Gratitude amplifies my glow. Joy flows through my thankful heart.

Glow-Up Challenge: End your day by writing down three specific things that made you smile or feel seen by God.

Rooted in Christ

Day 43
Water What's Working

February 12

"Let us not grow weary in doing good, for at the proper time we will reap a harvest if we do not give up."
Galatians 6:9

You don't need to start over you just need to keep watering what's working. Faith grows through daily devotion, not constant reinvention. Stay steady. Your harvest is forming.

Affirmation: I am consistent in the little things, and God is faithful in the big ones.

Glow-Up Challenge: Take note of one habit or rhythm that's been bearing fruit, thank God for it and keep watering it today.

Rooted in Christ

Day 44
Rooted in Hope

February 13

"May the God of hope fill you with all joy and peace as you trust in Him."
Romans 15:13

Hope is holy. It keeps your spirit alive when circumstances try to dim your faith. Hope is the whisper that says, "Keep believing. God's not finished yet."

Affirmation: My hope is rooted in God's faithfulness, not my feelings.

Glow-Up Challenge: Write down one area of your life that needs renewed hope. Pray over it and speak, "Lord, I trust You still."

Rooted in Christ

Day 45
Faithful in the Ordinary

February 14

"Do not despise these small beginnings, for the Lord rejoices to see the work begin."
Zechariah 4:10

Your glow grows in the ordinary moments, like folding laundry, driving the kids, showing up in love when no one sees. God finds glory in your quiet faithfulness.

Affirmation: I honor the sacred in my ordinary. God is present in my every day.

Glow-Up Challenge: Do one daily task prayerfully, turning it into an act of worship instead of a chore.

Rooted in Christ

Day 46
Let Your Light Be Love

February 15

"If we love one another, God lives in us and His love is made complete in us."
1 John 4:12

You don't have to preach to shine. Sometimes your kindness is the sermon. Every word, smile, or gesture rooted in love reveals the light of Christ.

Affirmation: My love is my light. I reflect God's heart through compassion.

Glow-Up Challenge: Do one unexpected act of love today, for a friend, stranger, or even yourself.

Rooted in Christ

Day 47
Rooted in Purpose

February 16

"For we are God's masterpiece, created in Christ Jesus to do good works."
Ephesians 2:10

You weren't created by accident. Your gifts, story, and struggles are all part of your divine design. Purpose isn't something you chase. It's something you remember.

Affirmation: I am God's masterpiece, walking boldly in my purpose.

Glow-Up Challenge: Reflect on one passion or gift that lights you up. Ask God how He wants to use it this week.

Rooted in Christ

Day 48
Keep Your Soil Soft

February 17

"Break up your unplowed ground; for it is time to seek the Lord."
Hosea 10:12

A hardened heart can't absorb new growth. Stay tender: open to correction, love, and new beginnings. God can plant miracles in soft soil.

Affirmation: My heart remains soft and teachable. I'm open to divine growth.

Glow-Up Challenge: Spend a few quiet minutes journaling, "Lord, where have I closed off my heart? Soften me again."

Rooted in Christ

Day 49
Steady in the Stretch

February 18

"I can do all things through Christ who strengthens me."
Philippians 4:13

Growth stretches you. Don't confuse stretching with breaking. It's how God expands your capacity. You are stronger than you think because He's strengthening you daily.

Affirmation: I am strengthened, stretched, and sustained by Christ within me.

Glow-Up Challenge: When you face something uncomfortable today, say, "This stretch is shaping me." Then move forward with grace.

Rooted in Christ

Day 50
Grow Slow, Glow Steady

February 19

"Be still in the presence of the Lord, and wait patiently for Him to act."
Psalm 37:7

Fast growth fades, but steady roots last. God's timing never rushes, and His blessings are never late. Your glow-up is not a race, it's a rhythm of trust.

Affirmation: I'm growing at God's pace, not the world's.

Glow-Up Challenge: Take a social media fast or break for one hour today and thank God for the pace of your own journey.

Rooted in Christ

Day 51
Anchored in His Word

February 20

"The grass withers and the flowers fade, but the Word of our God stands forever."
Isaiah 40:8

Everything changes, but God's Word remains. When your emotions shift, anchor your heart to His promises, they never move, even when life does.

Affirmation: My heart is anchored in the unchanging Word of God.

Glow-Up Challenge: Highlight or write down one verse that brings you peace and read it aloud before bed tonight.

Rooted in Christ

Day 52
Hidden Growth Is Holy

February 21

"Night and day, whether he sleeps or gets up, the seed sprouts and grows, though he does not know how."
Mark 4:27

You don't always have to see the growth to believe it's happening. God is working in hidden places, shaping you in silence, growing your roots in secret.

Affirmation: Even when I can't see progress, God is producing growth beneath the surface.

Glow-Up Challenge: Celebrate something unseen, thank God for the quiet growth happening in your life.

Rooted in Christ

Day 53
Choose Peace Over Pressure

February 22

"Peace I leave with you; My peace I give to you. Do not let your hearts be troubled."

John 14:27

Pressure says "hurry." Peace says "be still." The glow of peace outlasts the rush of performance. You were never meant to earn love, only receive it.

Affirmation: I release pressure and receive peace. I am held, not hurried.

Glow-Up Challenge: When you feel rushed, take one deep breath and say, "God, slow me down to Your pace."

Rooted in Christ

Day 54
Faithful Roots Bear Fruit

February 23

"The fruit of the Spirit is love, joy, peace, patience, kindness, goodness, faithfulness, gentleness, and self-control."
Galatians 5:22–23

Fruit grows from rooted faithfulness. Not perfection, but persistence. The more you stay planted in Him, the more His Spirit naturally shines through you.

Affirmation: I bear good fruit because I am rooted in His Spirit.

Glow-Up Challenge: Choose one fruit of the Spirit to intentionally practice today, maybe kindness, patience, or gentleness.

Rooted in Christ

Day 55
Rooted in Grace

February 24

"My grace is sufficient for you, for My power is made perfect in weakness."
2 Corinthians 12:9

Grace grows where striving ends. You don't have to be perfect to be powerful. God's strength shines best through surrendered hearts.

Affirmation: Grace covers me, carries me, and grows me.

Glow-Up Challenge: Instead of criticizing yourself today, speak grace: "I'm growing, and that's enough."

Rooted in Christ

Day 56
The Beauty of Becoming

February 25

"He saved us through the washing of rebirth and renewal by the Holy Spirit."
Titus 3:5

Becoming who God created you to be is a process, not a single moment. Transformation takes time, and every renewed thought is a step closer to the woman you're meant to be.

Affirmation: I'm not behind. I'm becoming.

Glow-Up Challenge: Write down one mindset you're ready to release, and one truth you'll replace it with.

Rooted in Christ

Day 57
Steady in the Unknown

February 26

"Trust in the Lord with all your heart and lean not on your own understanding."
Proverbs 3:5-6

Faith means standing firm even when you don't have the map. God isn't asking you to figure it out, He's asking you to follow.

Affirmation: I trust God even when I don't understand His plan.

Glow-Up Challenge: Write "Trust Over Understanding" on a sticky note and keep it somewhere you'll see it all week.

Rooted in Christ

Day 58
Rooted in Resilience

February 27

"Blessed is the one who perseveres under trial."
James 1:12

Every storm you've survived became soil for your strength. Resilience doesn't mean pretending you're fine, it means you keep showing up anyway, because your roots run deep.

❧

Affirmation: I am resilient in spirit and rooted in faith.

Glow-Up Challenge: Reflect on one trial you've overcome and thank God for the strength you discovered there.

Rooted in Christ

Day 59
Refreshed by Grace

February 28

"He refreshes my soul; He guides me along the right paths for His name's sake."
Psalm 23:3

When you feel weary, remember: God doesn't just restore you, He re-routes you back to peace. Grace isn't just a covering. It's a refill.

Affirmation: God's grace revives my soul and realigns my steps.

Glow-Up Challenge: Take 10 minutes today to rest in quiet prayer, no requests, just receiving His refreshing presence.

Rooted in Christ

Day 60
Rooted and Renewed

March 1

"Though outwardly we are wasting away, yet inwardly we are becoming renewed day by day."
2 Corinthians 4:16

You've made it to Day 60. Look how your roots have grown! You've learned to trust through waiting, to find peace in pauses, and to nourish your faith daily. This is your renewal season. You are still rooted, but ready to rise.

Affirmation: My roots are deep, my faith is steady, and my spirit is renewed.

Glow-Up Challenge: Journal a letter to God titled "My First 60 Days." Thank Him for every lesson that has strengthened your roots.

Rooted in Christ

Day 61
Refocus and Recenter

March 2

"Turn my eyes from worthless things and give me life through Your Word."
Psalm 119:37

Distractions are the weeds of the soul. Pull them up with truth and replace them with purpose. When you refocus on what matters, peace returns to your garden.

❧

Affirmation: My focus is fixed on what is holy and life-giving.

Glow-Up Challenge: Unplug for an hour today and do something that feeds your spirit instead of your scroll.

Rooted in Christ

Day 62
Let Faith Lead

March 3

"Let us fix our eyes on Jesus, the pioneer and perfector of faith."
Hebrews 12:2

When life feels uncertain, let faith take the wheel. You don't have to see the finish line to trust the One who charted the course.

Affirmation: I walk by faith, not by sight. My steps follow Jesus.

Glow-Up Challenge: Say a simple prayer before each task today: "Jesus, lead me through this."

Rooted in Christ

Day 63
Peace That Stays

March 4

"Whatever you have learned or received or heard from me, put it into practice. And the God of peace will be with you."
Philippians 4:9

Peace is a practice, not a moment. It stays when you keep putting faith into action: trusting, forgiving, loving, and resting in God's unshakable presence.

Affirmation: Peace is my default setting. God dwells within me.

Glow-Up Challenge: Take a slow, peaceful walk and thank God for every good thing you notice along the way.

Rooted in Christ

Day 64
Rooted in Patience

March 5

"Wait for the Lord and keep His way."
Psalm 37:34

Patience isn't passive. It's trust in motion. Every time you wait with faith instead of fear, your roots stretch deeper into peace.

Affirmation: I wait with grace and trust God's perfect timing.

Glow-Up Challenge: When you feel rushed or frustrated today, pause and whisper, "Lord, I trust Your timing more than my timeline."

Rooted in Christ

Day 65
Protect Your Peace

March 6

"In Me you may have peace. In this world you will have trouble. But take heart; I have overcome the world."
John 16:33

Peace is a promise, not a luxury. Guard it like treasure. You can't control what happens around you, but you can choose what you allow inside your spirit.

Affirmation: I protect my peace and keep my heart centered on Christ.

Glow-Up Challenge: Identify one thing that regularly steals your peace and set a boundary around it this week.

Rooted in Christ

Day 66
Stay Rooted in Joy

March 7

"You make known to me the path of life; in Your presence there is fullness of joy."
Psalm 16:11

Joy isn't about circumstance it's about closeness. When your heart stays close to God, joy becomes your natural glow.

Affirmation: My joy overflows from the presence of God within me.

Glow-Up Challenge: Do one joyful thing today: laugh, sing, dance, or create and dedicate it to God as worship.

Rooted in Christ

Day 67
The Strength of Stillness

March 8

"The Lord will fight for you; you need only to be still."
Exodus 14:14

Stillness doesn't mean inaction. It means surrender. Some battles are won when you stop striving and let God step in.

Affirmation: My stillness invites God's strength to move on my behalf.

Glow-Up Challenge: Set aside five quiet minutes today to breathe and repeat: "God, I trust You to fight for me."

Rooted in Christ

Day 68
Stay Planted in Faith

March 9

"Let us hold tightly without wavering to the hope we affirm, for God can be trusted to keep His promise."
Hebrews 10:23

Faith doesn't depend on evidence. It depends on endurance. Stay planted, even when you don't yet see the fruit. God is faithful, and His promises never expire.

Affirmation: My faith is planted deep. I trust God even when I can't see the outcome.

Glow-Up Challenge: Write down one promise of God that you're standing on. Read it every morning this week.

Rooted in Christ

Day 69
Nourished by Community

March 10

*"Two are better than one... if either of them falls down,
one can help the other up."*
Ecclesiastes 4:9–10

Roots intertwine underground. So do we. You weren't meant to grow alone, community strengthens your faith when life tries to uproot you.

Affirmation: I am surrounded by love, supported by faith, and strengthened through community.

Glow-Up Challenge: Reach out to a friend or sister in Christ today, send her encouragement, a prayer, or a verse that's helped you this week.

Rooted in Christ

Day 70
The Fruit of Faithfulness

March 11

"Well done, good and faithful servant."
Matthew 25:23

Faithfulness doesn't seek applause. It seeks alignment. Every time you stay rooted when you could have run, Heaven takes notice. God honors consistency, not perfection.

Affirmation: My quiet faithfulness bears fruit in due time.

Glow-Up Challenge: Reflect on one area where you've stayed faithful despite challenges. Thank God for sustaining your strength.

Rooted in Christ

Day 71
Rooted and Ready

March 12

"Then Christ will make His home in your heart as you trust in Him. Your roots will grow down into God's love and keep you strong."
Ephesians 3:17

You've grown deeper through God's nourishing presence, leaving the noise behind. Now, your foundation is firm. You're not who you were when you started. You're steadier, softer, and stronger in spirit.

Affirmation: I am rooted, built up, and ready to rise in faith.

Glow-Up Challenge: Write down one phrase that captures your growth during this phase, something you'll carry with you into the next season.

Rooted in Christ

Day 72
The Fruit of Gratitude

March 13

"I will give thanks to You, Lord, with all my heart; I will tell of all Your wonderful deeds."
Psalm 9:1

Gratitude turns your roots into rivers. When you thank God, you open the flow for blessings to move freely through your life. Gratitude shifts your energy, renews your peace, and strengthens your spirit.

Affirmation: Gratitude keeps my spirit glowing and my roots grounded.

Glow-Up Challenge: Make a gratitude list of ten blessings that came during this Rooted in Christ season, even the small, quiet ones.

Rooted in Christ

Day 73
Rise from the Roots

March 14

"They will be called oaks of righteousness, a planting of the Lord for the display of His splendor."
Isaiah 61:3

You've learned that your glow doesn't come from striving. It comes from staying planted in grace. The deeper the roots, the brighter the bloom. You are rising now refreshed and restored by grace.

Affirmation: I rise with peace, rooted in grace and radiant with purpose.

Glow-Up Challenge: Pray this short prayer: "Lord, thank You for the roots You've grown in me. Help me rise into healing, knowing I am grounded in You."

Rooted in Christ

Phase 1
Reflection
Rooted in Christ

You've done the holy work of planting your faith deep in the soil of God's truth.

This first season was about foundation learning that real growth begins beneath the surface, in the quiet surrender of your heart. You've discovered that being rooted doesn't mean you never shake. It means that even when the winds blow, your spirit stays grounded in grace.

You've practiced choosing faith over feelings, peace over perfection, and grace over guilt.

Your roots have stretched toward living water, the unshakable love of Christ, and they've found nourishment in stillness, Scripture, and trust.

Now, as you prepare to move into your next season of healing, pause and honor how far you've come. The same roots that held you steady will now draw up the healing you need for the journey ahead.

You are planted in purpose and prepared for restoration.

Rooted in Christ

Journal Prompts

What truths have taken root in my heart during this phase?

How has my understanding of faith, peace, or trust deepened?

Where have I seen God's hand steady me in unexpected ways?

What do I want to carry forward as I enter my healing season?

Rooted in Christ

Prayer

Lord, thank You for rooting me in Your Word and grounding my heart in Your peace. May the roots of my faith grow deeper with every season that comes.
Prepare my spirit for the healing ahead, and remind me that all growth begins in Your presence.
Amen.

Affirmation

I am rooted in Christ: grounded, growing, and ready to be healed from within.

Phase 2

Healed from Within

"Now that your roots have settled deep in faith, it's time to let God begin the healing that grows from within."

Healing is holy work.
It's the moment when your roots, now deep and steady, begin to draw in divine nourishment from the Source Himself. Healing doesn't mean erasing the past, it means inviting God into the places that still need His presence.

This phase is where transformation deepens. It's where forgiveness softens what was hardened, and grace begins to replace the weight of shame. It's the work that happens beneath the glow, where you remember that wholeness isn't something you earn. It's something you receive.

Let God lead the way in this next part of your Holy Glow-Up. Let Him touch the tender places and restore what's been weary.
Because healing isn't just about becoming whole, it's about remembering that you already are, in Him.

Healed from Within

Day 74
Healing Begins with Honesty

March 15

"The Lord is close to the brokenhearted and saves those who are crushed in spirit."
Psalm 34:18

You can't heal what you hide. Honesty opens the door for grace to walk in. God doesn't need your perfection. He just wants your truth.

Affirmation: My healing begins when I show up honestly before God.

Glow-Up Challenge: Write one thing you've been carrying quietly, and hand it over to God in prayer tonight.

Healed from Within

Day 75
Let the Light In

March 16

"The light shines in the darkness, and the darkness has not overcome it."
John 1:5

God's light isn't afraid of your darkness. He enters gently, illuminating every wound with compassion, not condemnation. Healing happens when you stop hiding and start inviting Him in.

Affirmation: I welcome God's healing light into every part of my being.

Glow-Up Challenge: Light a candle today as a symbol of invitation, a physical reminder that God's light dwells within you.

Healed from Within

Day 76
The Beauty of Brokenness

March 17

"He heals the brokenhearted and binds up their wounds."
Psalm 147:3

Your cracks don't make you unworthy, they make you human. And in God's hands, even the shattered pieces become sacred art. Healing doesn't erase your story, it redeems it.

Affirmation: My brokenness is becoming beauty in God's hands.

Glow-Up Challenge: Write one part of your story you've tried to hide and thank God for how He's using it to shape your strength.

Healed from Within

Day 77
Forgive to Be Free

March 18

"Bear with each other and forgive one another if any of you has a grievance against someone. Forgive as the Lord forgave you."
Colossians 3:13

Forgiveness isn't saying what happened was okay. It's saying, "I'm done letting it control me." Freedom blooms when you choose release over resentment.

Affirmation: I forgive so I can live free.

Glow-Up Challenge: Write a forgiveness letter. You don't have to send it. Let it be your release and surrender.

Healed from Within

Day 78
Healing Takes Time

March 19

"See! The winter is past; the rains are over and gone. Flowers appear on the earth; the season of singing has come, the cooing of doves is heard in our land."
Song of Solomon 2:11-12

Don't rush the recovery. Healing is not linear. Some days you'll feel whole, and others you'll feel raw again. God is patient with your process. You can be, too.

Affirmation: I give myself grace to heal at God's pace.

Glow-Up Challenge: Rest intentionally today. Your stillness is not wasted. It's working.

Healed from Within

Day 79
God Heals Through People

March 20

"As iron sharpens iron, so one person sharpens another."
Proverbs 27:17

Sometimes healing arrives through a conversation, a hug, or a sister who simply listens. God often sends people as answers to prayers you never spoke aloud.

Affirmation: I am open to receive healing through divine connections.

Glow-Up Challenge: Reach out to someone who's been on your heart. God may be using that connection for both your healing.

Healed from Within

Day 80
Wholeness Over Wounds

March 21

"He has sent me to bind up the brokenhearted... to proclaim freedom for the captives."
Isaiah 61:1

You are not your wound. You are the one God chose to rise from it. Healing doesn't erase the scar. It redefines it as a mark of victory.

Affirmation: I am whole, healed, and walking in freedom.

Glow-Up Challenge: Speak this out loud: "I am healed, I am whole, and I am His."

Healed from Within

Day 81
Healing Through Surrender

March 22

"Cast all your anxiety on Him because He cares for you."
1 Peter 5:7

Healing begins when you stop trying to fix yourself and start letting God do what only He can. Surrender isn't giving up, it's giving over.

Affirmation: I release control and rest in God's healing hands.

Glow-Up Challenge: Write down one thing you're trying to control and say aloud, "God, I trust You with this."

Healed from Within

Day 82
The Power of Compassion

March 23

"Clothe yourselves with compassion, kindness, humility, gentleness, and patience."
Colossians 3:12

Be gentle with yourself. Healing isn't about perfection. It's about compassion. Speak to yourself like someone you're caring for, not correcting.

Affirmation: I treat myself with grace, love, and compassion.

Glow-Up Challenge: When self-criticism rises today, replace it with, "God's still working on me, and I'm worthy in the process."

Healed from Within

Day 83
The Healing of Letting Go

March 24

*"Forget the former things; do not dwell on the past.
See, I am doing a new thing!"
Isaiah 43:18–19*

You can't step into the new while gripping the old. Letting go isn't losing. It's clearing space for better things to grow. God's new thing is waiting for you to release what's run its course.

Affirmation: I let go with grace, making space for new blessings to bloom.

Glow-Up Challenge: Write down one thing you're releasing and tear or burn the paper safely as a symbolic act of freedom.

Healed from Within

Day 84
Healing the Inner Dialogue

March 25

"The tongue has the power of life and death."
Proverbs 18:21

What you speak to yourself matters. Healing begins when your words match God's truth, when you stop repeating the lies of the past and start declaring the promises of your future.

Affirmation: My words carry healing. I speak life over myself.

Glow-Up Challenge: Look in the mirror and say five loving truths about yourself out loud.

Healed from Within

Day 85
God's Love Restores Worth

March 26

"Nothing can separate us from the love of God."
Romans 8:38–39

You were never unworthy, just unaware of your worth. God's love doesn't need you to earn it. It invites you to receive it. His love restores what rejection once took.

Affirmation: I am fully known, fully loved, and fully worthy in Christ.

Glow-Up Challenge: Write "I am loved and chosen by God" somewhere visible as your reminder today.

Healed from Within

Day 86
Healing Through Worship

March 27

"Worship the Lord with gladness; come before Him with joyful songs."
Psalm 100:2

Worship is medicine for the soul. It shifts your focus from pain to praise, reminding you that healing flows when gratitude opens the heart.

Affirmation: My worship invites healing; my praise is my power.

Glow-Up Challenge: Play a worship song that moves you. Sing it loud, and let your soul exhale.

Healed from Within

Day 87
Rewriting the Story

March 28

"Be made new in that attitude of your minds; and put on the new self, created to be like God in true righteousness and holiness."
Ephesians 4:23-24

Healing means refusing to live as the old you when God has already made you new. You are not your past. You're the living proof of God's redemptive power.

Affirmation: I am walking in my new chapter, healed and whole.

Glow-Up Challenge: Journal your "new story". Who are you becoming in this season of restoration?

Healed from Within

Day 88
Healing Through Trust

March 29

"Blessed is the one who trusts in the Lord, whose confidence is in Him."
Jeremiah 17:7

Healing doesn't happen through control. It happens through trust. When you stop replaying what hurt you and start relying on who heals you, peace takes root.

Affirmation: I trust the One who holds every piece of my healing.

Glow-Up Challenge: Each time worry rises today, whisper, "I trust You, Lord," until peace returns.

Healed from Within

Day 89
The Soft Strength of Grace

March 30

"We have this treasure in jars of clay to show that this all-surpassing power is from God and not from us."
2 Corinthians 4:7

Grace doesn't harden you. It strengthens you softly. It gives you the courage to feel without fear and to grow without guilt. Strength doesn't always roar. Sometimes it rests.

Affirmation: I walk in soft strength. Grace is my armor and peace is my posture.

Glow-Up Challenge: Let yourself rest today without apology. Healing thrives in stillness.

Healed from Within

Day 90
Boundaries Are Healing Too

March 31

"Like a city whose walls are broken through a person who lacks self-control."
Proverbs 25:28

Boundaries aren't walls. They're gates that let love flow in healthy ways. Healing means recognizing what drains your peace and protecting your spirit without guilt.

Affirmation: My boundaries are sacred. They protect my peace and preserve my joy.

Glow-Up Challenge: Write down one boundary you need to strengthen and one that's been life-giving. Thank God for both.

Healed from Within

Day 91
Healing Through Acceptance

April 1

"I have learned to be content whatever the circumstances."
Philippians 4:11

Acceptance isn't giving up. It's giving God permission to use your present moment. Peace comes when you stop resisting what is and start trusting what's being built through it.

Affirmation: I accept this season with grace, knowing God is working through it.

Glow-Up Challenge: Journal about something you're learning to accept, and thank God for the hidden blessings in it.

Healed from Within

Day 92
The Freedom of Forgiving Yourself

April 2

"You will again have compassion on us; You will tread our sins underfoot and hurl all our iniquities into the depths of the sea."
Micah 7:19

Self-forgiveness is sacred. God already released what you're still holding against yourself. Healing requires you to stop punishing yourself for what grace already covered.

Affirmation: I forgive myself fully. I walk freely in grace.

Glow-Up Challenge: Look in the mirror today and say, "I release myself. I am forgiven. I am free."

Healed from Within

Day 93
Healing Through Gratitude

April 3

"Do not be anxious about anything, but in every situation, by prayer and petition, with Thanksgiving, present your request to God."
Philippians 4:6

Thankfulness shifts the frequency of the heart. Gratitude turns wounds into wisdom and pain into perspective. The more you thank Him, the lighter healing feels.

Affirmation: Gratitude is my daily medicine. I find healing in thanksgiving.

Glow-Up Challenge: List five things that remind you God is still good, even in the middle of your healing.

Healed from Within

Day 94
Restored from the Inside Out

April 4

"I will restore to you the years that the locust has eaten."
Joel 2:25

God restores what was lost. Your restoration may look different, but it's always complete. Healing from within means letting His Spirit rebuild your peace, renew your joy, and reawaken your hope.

Affirmation: I am restored from the inside out. God is making all things new in me.

Glow-Up Challenge: Reflect on how you've changed since starting this phase. Write one word that defines your restoration so far.

Healed from Within

Day 95
The Peace of Perspective

April 5

"And we know that in all things God works for the good of those who love Him."
Romans 8:28

Healing often comes through hindsight. What once hurt now holds meaning. God never wastes pain. He repurposes it into wisdom that shapes your next chapter.

Affirmation: I trust that every piece of my past is being used for purpose.

Glow-Up Challenge: Reflect on one hardship that eventually worked out for your good. Write what it taught you about God's faithfulness.

Healed from Within

Day 96
Healing Through Humility

April 6

"Humble yourselves before the Lord, and He will lift you up."
James 4:10

Healing isn't about pride or performance. It's about surrender. Humility opens the heart to divine help, allowing God to lift you higher than your own strength ever could.

Affirmation: I bow before God in humility and rise through His grace.

Glow-Up Challenge: Pray this today: "Lord, remove my need to appear strong and teach me to rely on You."

Healed from Within

Day 97
The Restoration of Rest

April 7

"You will find rest for your souls."
Matthew 11:29

Rest is part of recovery. The world may call it laziness, but Heaven calls it healing. In your rest, God restores energy, clarity, and joy.

Affirmation: Rest renews me. I honor the holy rhythm of pause and peace.

Glow-Up Challenge: Take a nap, a walk, or a quiet moment of worship, and release the guilt that says you have to "do more."

Healed from Within

Day 98
Healing the Mind

April 8

"Be transformed by the renewing of your mind."
Romans 12:2

True healing starts in thought. When you replace the lies you believed with the truth God speaks, you change the way your whole life feels.

Affirmation: My mind is renewed daily by truth and peace.

Glow-Up Challenge: Catch one negative thought today and replace it with a declaration of faith. An example could be, "I am healed. I am loved. I am whole."

Healed from Within

Day 99
Redeemed by Grace

April 9

"He gave Himself to redeem us from all wickedness and to purify for Himself a people that are His very own."
Titus 2:14

You don't have to rewrite your past. Grace already did. Redemption means God took every wrong turn and wove it into your divine direction.

Affirmation: My past is redeemed, my present is peaceful, and my future is blessed.

Glow-Up Challenge: Write this prayer in your journal: "Thank You, Lord, that nothing I've been through is wasted in Your hands."

Healed from Within

Day 100
Healing Through Hope

April 10

"As for me, I will always have hope; I will praise You more and more."
Psalm 71:14

Hope is healing's heartbeat. It's what keeps your spirit alive when your circumstances haven't caught up yet. Hope whispers, "God's not finished."

Affirmation: My hope is unbreakable because it's built on His promise.

Glow-Up Challenge: Write down one thing you're hopeful for, and instead of asking if, thank God for when.

Healed from Within

Day 101
Wholeness is a Journey

April 11

"The Lord will fulfill His purpose for me; Your steadfast love, O Lord, endures forever."
Psalm 138:8

Healing isn't a one-time miracle. It's a daily journey of grace. You are becoming whole in every area of your life, and God is faithful to finish what He started.

Affirmation: I am a continual work of healing and grace. God's work in me is not done.

Glow-Up Challenge: Reflect on your growth so far. Whisper this prayer: "Lord, thank You for healing me layer by layer."

Healed from Within

Day 102
Healing Through Peace

April 12

"Again Jesus said, 'Peace be with you! As the Father has sent me, I am sending you.'"
John 20:21

Peace isn't found. It's chosen. The world offers temporary calm. God gives lasting peace that settles your spirit even when life doesn't make sense.

Affirmation: I am surrounded and sustained by divine peace.

Glow-Up Challenge: When stress arises today, pause and take three deep breaths. Say aloud, "Peace is already within me."

Healed from Within

Day 103
You Are Not What Happened

April 13

"If anyone is in Christ, they are a new creation; the old has gone, the new has come!"
2 Corinthians 5:17

Your identity isn't rooted in what broke you, but in the One who rebuilt you. Healing means releasing labels that pain tried to stick to your soul.

Affirmation: I am not defined by what hurt me. I am defined by what healed me.

Glow-Up Challenge: Write down three new words that describe who you are becoming. Speak them over yourself throughout the day.

Healed from Within

Day 104
Healing Through Truth

April 14

"Then you will know the truth, and the truth will set you free."
John 8:32

Healing often begins with honesty, especially with yourself. Truth may sting at first, but it sets the foundation for real freedom. Let God's truth replace your inner narrative with love.

Affirmation: I walk in truth and live in freedom.

Glow-Up Challenge: Ask God to reveal one truth you need to embrace today. And one lie you're ready to release.

Healed from Within

Day 105
Letting Love Lead

April 15

"Do everything in love."
1 Corinthians 16:14

Love is the language of healing. When you let love lead in how you speak, respond, and think, you align your heart with Heaven.

Affirmation: Love leads me. Grace guides me.

Glow-Up Challenge: Choose to respond in love today, especially in a situation where you'd normally react in frustration.

Healed from Within

Day 106
The Power of Presence

April 16

"God is our refuge and strength, an ever-present help in trouble."
Psalm 46:1

God's healing presence is not distant. It's here, right now. Healing deepens when you slow down enough to feel His nearness in your ordinary moments.

Affirmation: God's presence is my refuge. I am never alone in my healing.

Glow-Up Challenge: Set aside five minutes today to do nothing but sit with God. No words, no requests, just presence.

Healed from Within

Day 107
Beauty in Becoming

April 17

"The end of a matter is better than its beginning, and patience is better than pride."
Ecclesiastes 7:8

Healing is not about who you were. It's about who you're becoming. Beauty unfolds when you trust the process, even when it's messy. Becoming is the sacred art of letting God reveal your next layer.

Affirmation: I am becoming more whole, more radiant, and more like Him each day.

Glow-Up Challenge: Write down one area where you've seen beauty emerge from something broken.

Healed from Within

Day 108
The Calm After the Storm

April 18

"You turned my mourning into dancing; You removed my sackcloth and clothed me with joy."
Psalm 30:11

There comes a point in healing when peace feels natural again. That's the moment you realize you didn't just survive. You were transformed.

Affirmation: My peace is proof of God's healing power in me.

Glow-Up Challenge: Play a song that feels like joy and let yourself smile. Even if the healing isn't finished, the joy has begun.

Healed from Within

Day 109
Healing Through Faithfulness

April 19

"Because of the Lord's great love we are not consumed... His compassions never fail. They are new every morning."
Lamentations 3:22–23

Healing is built on consistency and showing up each day, even when you don't feel strong. God's mercies renew daily. Your healing does, too.

Affirmation: I am faithful in my healing, and God is faithful to complete it.

Glow-Up Challenge: Begin your morning with gratitude. Before checking your phone, thank God for three new mercies today.

Healed from Within

Day 110
The Gentle Work of God

April 20

"He tends His flock like a shepherd; He gathers the lambs in His arms and carries them close to Hia heart; He gently leads those that have young."
Isaiah 40:11

God's healing is gentle. He doesn't rush your recovery. He restores you softly, like water smoothing stone. Don't mistake gentleness for weakness. It's the way grace rebuilds strength.

Affirmation: God restores me gently and completely.

Glow-Up Challenge: Do something nurturing today. Take a slow walk, light a candle, or journal with soft worship music playing.

Healed from Within

Day 111
Healing Through Gratitude

April 21

"Oh give thanks to the Lord, for he is good, for his steadfast love endures forever."
Psalms 107:1

Gratitude is medicine for the soul. When you thank God in the middle of healing, it shifts your focus from what's missing to what's mending.

Affirmation: Gratitude grows my peace and nourishes my healing.

Glow-Up Challenge: Write a short thank-you letter to God for the ways He's healed you so far, big or small.

Healed from Within

Day 112
The Healing Power of Joy

April 22

"I have told you this so that My joy may be in you and that your joy may be complete."
John 15:11

Joy isn't just an emotion. It's a spiritual strength that recharges your heart. Every time you choose joy, you reclaim territory from pain.

Affirmation: My joy is strength, and my laughter is a form of praise.

Glow-Up Challenge: Do something playful or lighthearted today. Healing grows in laughter.

Healed from Within

Day 113
Healing from the Inside Out

April 23

"A cheerful heart is good medicine, but a crushed spirit dries up the bones."
Proverbs 17:22

Healing flows from the inside out: from your spirit to your emotions, and then to your body. When your heart is at peace, your whole being begins to glow.

Affirmation: My inner peace creates outer healing. I radiate divine wellness.

Glow-Up Challenge: Drink more water today. Each sip, whisper, "Lord, cleanse and renew me from the inside out."

Healed from Within

Day 114
The Strength of a Soft Heart

April 24

"I will remove your heart of stone and give you a heart of flesh."
Ezekiel 36:26

It takes strength to stay soft in a world that teaches hardness. God honors your tenderness. It's proof that you've been healed by love, not by bitterness.

Affirmation: My softness is not weakness. It's evidence of healing.

Glow-Up Challenge: Extend grace to someone who doesn't expect it. Softness multiplies when shared.

Healed from Within

Day 115
Fully Restored

April 25

"Restore to me the joy of Your salvation and grant me a willing spirit, to sustain me."
Psalm 51:12

You've walked through the valley, and now you're emerging in light. Restoration doesn't erase what happened. It transforms what it meant. This is where peace becomes your new normal: steady, sacred, and strong.

Affirmation: I am restored, renewed, and radiant in spirit.

Glow-Up Challenge: Write down three ways your heart feels lighter than when you began Healed from Within.

Healed from Within

Day 116
Healing Through Release

April 26

"Cast your cares on the Lord and He will sustain you."
Psalm 55:22

Release is the final stage of healing. It's the holy exhale. Every time you hand your worries to God, your heart gets lighter, and your faith grows stronger.

Affirmation: I release all that weighs me down and rest in divine peace.

Glow-Up Challenge: Write down your biggest current worry on a piece of paper, fold it, and pray, "Lord, I give this to You completely." Then throw it away.

Healed from Within

Day 117
The Courage to Feel Again

April 27

"This is what the Sovereign Lord says to these bones: I will make breath enter you, and you will come to life."
Ezekiel 37:5

Healing isn't about avoiding emotion. It's about letting God breathe life into what went numb. Feeling again is a sign that your heart is coming back to life.

Affirmation: I am safe to feel, and my emotions are being healed by grace.

Glow-Up Challenge: Allow yourself to feel whatever comes up today joy, sadness, gratitude and invite God into that feeling.

Healed from Within

Day 118
The Lightness of Letting Go

April 28

"Do not worry about tomorrow, for tomorrow will worry about itself."
Matthew 6:34

When you let go of control, peace finds space to enter. Healing makes you lighter because you're no longer carrying what wasn't yours to hold.

Affirmation: I live free and light. I trust God with every tomorrow.

Glow-Up Challenge: End your day by thanking God for three burdens you no longer carry.

Healed from Within

Day 119
Healed Hearts Heal Others

April 29

"He comforts us in all our troubles so that we can comfort those in any trouble."
2 Corinthians 1:4

Your healing has a purpose beyond you. The peace you've found becomes the balm you'll share. When you speak from healed places, others find hope in your light.

Affirmation: My healing carries hope for others. I am a vessel of comfort and grace.

Glow-Up Challenge: Send an encouraging text, prayer, or verse to someone who might need the same reminder you once did.

Healed from Within

Day 120
Whole and Holy

April 30

"I pray that you may enjoy good health and that all may go well with you, even as your soul is getting along well."
3 John 1:2

You've completed your season of inner restoration. Your heart is whole, your spirit is steady, and your glow is no longer from striving. It's from divine alignment.
Healing wasn't the destination. Wholeness is.

Affirmation: I am whole, healed, and walking in holy alignment with God's purpose.

Glow-Up Challenge: Stand in front of a mirror today, place your hand over your heart, and declare: "God, thank You for healing me from within."

Healed from Within

Phase 2
Reflection

Healed and Whole

Take a deep breath, beautiful soul.
You've walked through one of the most sacred parts of your Holy Glow-Up. The season where healing took root and peace began to grow in places once filled with pain.

These past weeks weren't easy, but they were holy. You've learned to surrender what you couldn't fix, forgive what once broke you, and open your heart again to God's gentle touch.

Your healing isn't a chapter that ends. It's a foundation that will steady you for every season to come. You're no longer living from your wounds. You're living from your wholeness.

You are the living proof that God restores, renews, and redeems every story.

Let this be your moment to exhale, to honor the strength it took to stay soft, the courage it took to keep believing, and the faith it took to heal from within.

Healed from Within

Journal Prompts

What has God healed or softened in me during this phase?

How do I feel different emotionally, spiritually, or mentally than when I began?

What truths now anchor my peace?

How can I use my healing to help others around me?

Healed from Within

Prayer

Lord, thank You for walking with me through this season of inner healing. You have turned my pain into purpose and my tears into testimony.
Help me carry this peace into every new challenge ahead. May my healed heart reflect Your light wherever I go.
Amen.

Affirmation
I am healed, whole, and free. I am glowing with the peace that only God can give.

Phase 3

Glow Through the Storm

You've found peace in stillness. Now, it's time to shine through movement. The glow that was born in healing will now carry you through life's winds and rains.

Phase 3 is where your faith gets tested, not to break you, but to reveal how strong your roots have become. You'll learn that storms don't dim your light. They deepen it. You'll discover that joy can still rise in the middle of hardship, and that your glow isn't fragile. It's fortified.

You are no longer the seed learning to grow. You're the flower that knows she can stand in the rain.

This next phase isn't about avoiding storms. It's about glowing through them.

Day 121
Glowing in the Rain

May 1

"Consider it pure joy, my brothers and sisters, whenever you face trials of many kinds, because you know that the testing of your faith produces perseverance."
James 1:2–3

The glow that lasts is born in the storm. Every challenge becomes a chance to prove your light is real. It is not surface-deep, but soul-strong.

Affirmation: My faith glows brightest when the rain falls.

Glow-Up Challenge: Instead of asking "why me?" today, ask, "what's God growing in me?"

Glow Through the Storm

Day 122
Anchored in the Waves

May 2

"We have this hope as an anchor for the soul, firm and secure."
Hebrews 6:19

When the winds rise, remember your anchor. It's not in the situation. It's in the Savior. Hope keeps you grounded when emotions want to drift.

Affirmation: My hope is anchored in God. I will not be moved.

Glow-Up Challenge: Draw or write your "anchor verse". A Scripture that steadies you when life feels unsteady.

Glow Through the Storm

Day 123
Finding Calm in Chaos

May 3

"He got up, rebuked the wind and said to the waves, 'Peace! Be still!' And the wind died down and it was completely calm."
Mark 4:39

Peace isn't the absence of storms. It's the presence of Jesus in the middle of them. When everything feels uncertain, breathe in His peace and know He still commands the waves.

Affirmation: I carry calm within because Jesus is in my boat.

Glow-Up Challenge: When stress hits today, pause and whisper, "Peace, be still." Watch what happens in your spirit.

Glow Through the Storm

Day 124
Strength in the Struggle

May 4

"It is God who arms me with strength and keeps my way secure."
Psalm 18:23-33

Embracing your glow doesn't mean you won't struggle. It means you'll shine through it. Every difficulty becomes a divine gym where your faith gains muscle.

❧

Affirmation: I am strong in spirit. Struggle only strengthens my shine.

Glow-Up Challenge: Think of one past challenge you overcame. Thank God for the strength it built in you.

Glow Through the Storm

Day 125
Trusting Through the Unknown

May 5

"I will lead the blind by ways they have not known."
Isaiah 42:16

God's path often leads through uncertainty. You don't need to see the whole route. Just trust the One guiding each step. He knows the way even when you don't.

Affirmation: I walk by trust, not by sight. God lights my path one step at a time.

Glow-Up Challenge: Do one thing today that requires faith, not full understanding.

Glow Through the Storm

Day 126
Light in the Valley

May 6

"Even though I walk through the valley of the shadow of death, I will fear no evil, for You are with me."
Psalm 23:4

Your glow is not canceled by darkness. It's confirmed by it. The valley doesn't reflect defeat. It's the place where your faith finds its voice.

Affirmation: God's light leads me through every valley. Fear has no home here.

Glow-Up Challenge: Write a short declaration of faith for your next "valley moment." Keep it where you can see it.

Glow Through the Storm

Day 127
Joy in the Journey

May 7

"Yet I will rejoice in the Lord, I will be joyful in God my Savior."
Habakkuk 3:18

Joy isn't based on outcomes. It's a declaration. When you choose joy, even in hard seasons, you show the world what faith really looks like.

Affirmation: My joy is anchored in Jesus, not in circumstance.

Glow-Up Challenge: Smile on purpose today, not because life is perfect, but because God is present. Choose joy, regardless of circumstances.

Glow Through the Storm

Day 128
Steady in the Storm

May 8

"They are like a man building a house... Who dug down deep and laid the foundation on rock."
Luke 6:48

Storms reveal what's solid. You've built your life on the Rock. That means you might sway, but you won't shatter. The winds test your faith, but they also prove your foundation.

Affirmation: I am steady on the Rock. No storm can shake what God has built.

Glow-Up Challenge: Write down one time you thought you'd fall apart, and thank God for the strength that kept you standing.

Glow Through the Storm

Day 129
When You Feel Weary

May 9

"Never tire of doing what is good."
2 Thessalonians 3:13

Even warriors get tired. Healing, helping, and hoping take energy. God doesn't ask you to push through alone. He offers rest for the resilient.

Affirmation: I am allowed to rest. God renews my strength daily.

Glow-Up Challenge: Rest intentionally today nap, pray, breathe and let God refill what the storm drained.

Glow Through the Storm

Day 130
Finding Purpose in Pain

May 10

"The sufferings of this present time are not worth comparing with the glory that will be revealed in us."
Romans 8:18

Your pain isn't pointless. Every tear has been watering purpose. God never wastes hurt. He transforms it into the testimony someone else will need.

Affirmation: My pain is becoming purpose, and my story carries light.

Glow-Up Challenge: Reflect on one hard season and write what it taught you about God's faithfulness.

Glow Through the Storm

Day 131
The Power of Perseverance

May 11

"You need to persevere so that when you have done the will of God, you will receive what He has promised."
Hebrews 10:36

Breakthrough often comes right after the urge to quit. Perseverance isn't perfection. It's simply refusing to stop trusting.

Affirmation: I persevere with patience. God's promises are worth the wait.

Glow-Up Challenge: Encourage yourself out loud: "I'm closer than I think. God is not done yet."

Glow Through the Storm

Day 132
Faith Over Fear

May 12

"Do not fear, for I am with you... I will strengthen you and help you."
Isaiah 41:10

Fear whispers, "What if?" Faith answers, "Even if." God's presence is the antidote to anxiety. He is your calm within chaos.

Affirmation: Fear doesn't lead me. Faith does.

Glow-Up Challenge: When fear rises, pause and repeat: "Even if it rains, I will still shine."

Glow Through the Storm

Day 133
The Storm is Temporary

May 13

"Our present troubles are small and won't last very long... yet they produce for us a glory that vastly outweighs them."
2 Corinthians 4:17

The storm might feel endless, but it's not eternal. What's building in you will outlast what's breaking around you. Hold on. The light is already returning.

Affirmation: This storm is temporary. God's glory in me is permanent.

Glow-Up Challenge: Write down one thing you know won't last. And one eternal truth that will.

Glow Through the Storm

Day 134
Glow Anyway

May 14

"Believe in the light while you have the light, so that you may become children of light."
John 12:36

Your glow is not situational. It's spiritual. The storm doesn't define your shine. Your faith does. Glow anyway, because someone lost in their own storm needs your light to find hope.

Affirmation: I glow through every season. My faith shines brighter than fear.

Glow-Up Challenge: Share one word of encouragement or hope online or with someone in your life. Let your light ripple outward.

Glow Through the Storm

Day 135
Refined by Fire

May 15

"These trials will show that your faith is genuine. It is being tested as fire tests and purifies gold."
1 Peter 1:7

Storms don't destroy your light. They refine it. Every fire you walk through removes what's not needed, revealing the gold of your faith beneath the surface.

Affirmation: I am refined, not ruined, by what I've endured.

Glow-Up Challenge: Write down one hardship that revealed strength or wisdom you didn't know you had.

Glow Through the Storm

Day 136
When Prayers Feel Unanswered

May 16

"How long, Lord? Will You forget me forever?"
Psalm 13:1

Even the faithful wrestle with silence. When God seems quiet, it's not distance. It's development. He's strengthening your trust to hold the blessing when it comes.

Affirmation: God's silence is not His absence. He's still working in the waiting.

Glow-Up Challenge: Write a letter to God expressing what's on your heart, even if it's messy. He can handle your honesty.

Glow Through the Storm

Day 137
Grace in the Grit

May 17

"For to be sure, he was crucified in weakness, yet he lives by God's power. Likewise, we are weak in him, yet by God's power we will live with him."
2 Corinthians 13:4

Grace meets you in the middle of the mess. It's what carries you when your strength runs out. Healing taught you to rest. Now grace teaches you to endure.

Affirmation: I'm powered by grace, not by perfection.

Glow-Up Challenge: When frustration hits today, pause and say, "Grace, not grind."

Glow Through the Storm

Day 138
Praise Through Pressure

May 18

"I will bless the Lord at all times; His praise will always be on my lips."
Psalm 34:1

Worship in the storm is spiritual warfare. Praise shifts the atmosphere, reminding both Heaven and hell that your faith stands firm no matter what.

Affirmation: My praise is my power. It pushes back every shadow.

Glow-Up Challenge: Turn on a worship song when pressure rises. Lift your voice and let praise be your peace.

Glow Through the Storm

Day 139
Purpose in the Pause

May 19

"Do not be afraid. Stand firm and you will see the deliverance the Lord will bring you today."
Exodus 14:13

Not every pause is punishment. Sometimes it's protection. God uses pauses to redirect you toward something better, something prepared.

Affirmation: I trust God's pauses. They prepare me for His promises.

Glow-Up Challenge: Reflect on a time something didn't go as planned. How did it lead to something better later?

Glow Through the Storm

Day 140
The Glow of Obedience

May 20

"To obey is better than sacrifice."
1 Samuel 15:22

Obedience keeps your glow steady when life feels dark. It's not about control. It's about trust. Every "yes" to God, even when uncomfortable, keeps you aligned with purpose.

Affirmation: I choose obedience even when I don't understand the outcome.

Glow-Up Challenge: Say "yes" to one small nudge from God today, even if it scares you a little.

Glow Through the Storm

Day 141
Rainbows After Rain

May 21

"I have set my rainbow in the clouds, and it will be the sign of the covenant between Me and the earth."
Genesis 9:13

Every storm ends and every one leaves a reminder of God's covenant love. The rainbow isn't just in the sky. It's in you. Proof that grace remains after the rain.

Affirmation: I carry God's promise within me. Beauty always follows the storm.

Glow-Up Challenge: Step outside and notice something beautiful in creation. A sign that the storm has passed.

Glow Through the Storm

Day 142
Strength in the Stretch

May 22

"Enlarge the place of your tent… stretch your tent curtains wide, do not hold back."
Isaiah 54:2

Sometimes the storm stretches you so your capacity can expand. Growth isn't always comfortable, but it's always purposeful.

Affirmation: Every stretch makes me stronger. I'm growing beyond my limits.

Glow-Up Challenge: Identify one area where God might be stretching your faith. Instead of resisting, thank Him for the growth.

Glow Through the Storm

Day 143
The Calm of Confidence

May 23

"For it is God who works in you to will and to act in order to fulfill his good purpose."
Philippians 2:13

Confidence in Christ isn't arrogance. It's assurance. It's knowing the One who started your glow-up will finish it beautifully.

Affirmation: I'm confident in Christ, and calm because He's in control.

Glow-Up Challenge: Walk today with spiritual posture shoulders back, chin up, heart open knowing God's not done.

Glow Through the Storm

Day 144
Light in the Waiting

May 24

"The Lord is good to those whose hope is in Him… it is good to wait quietly for the salvation of the Lord."
Lamentations 3:25-26

Waiting is one of faith's greatest teachers. It tests your patience, but also proves your trust. Even when nothing seems to move, God is still making a way.

Affirmation: I wait well. Trusting God's timing more than my timeline.

Glow-Up Challenge: Spend 5 minutes journaling what you've learned from a season of waiting. Look for evidence of growth.

Glow Through the Storm

Day 145
Grace in the Grind

May 25

"Whatever you do, do it all for the glory of God."
1 Corinthians 10:31

Even in busy seasons, grace meets you. When you infuse your work with purpose, ordinary moments become sacred.

Affirmation: My daily work is worship. Grace fuels every effort.

Glow-Up Challenge: As you work today, whether at home, at your desk, or in errands, silently dedicate each task to God.

Glow Through the Storm

Day 146
Unshaken Peace

May 26

"The Lord gives strength to His people; the Lord blesses His people with peace."
Psalm 29:11

Peace isn't found in perfect conditions. It's found in perfect confidence that God has already won. Even when storms rage, your soul can stay still.

Affirmation: My peace is unshaken because it's rooted in victory, not circumstance.

Glow-Up Challenge: Each time worry comes today, whisper: "Jesus already overcame this."

Glow Through the Storm

Day 147
Glow Through Giving

May 27

"It is more blessed to give than to receive."
Acts 20:35

Even in storm seasons, generosity multiplies joy. Giving time, love, encouragement keeps your heart open and your spirit glowing.

Affirmation: I give freely. My generosity shines God's love into the world.

Glow-Up Challenge: Give something today a compliment, a prayer, a favor and watch how it fills you, too.

Glow Through the Storm

Day 148
The Still Glow

May 28

"The Lord your God is with you… He will rejoice over you with singing."
Zephaniah 3:17

When the storm finally settles, what remains is peace. Stillness is where your glow deepens through surrender comes breakthrough.

Affirmation: My stillness is sacred. My glow grows in God's quiet.

Glow-Up Challenge: Spend 10 minutes in silence today no distractions, no lists. Just rest in God's presence.

Glow Through the Storm

Day 149
When Faith Feels Fragile

May 29

"Lord, I believe; help my unbelief!"
Mark 9:24

Even strong faith wavers sometimes and that's okay. God never asks for perfection, just presence. The tiniest spark of belief still counts as light.

Affirmation: Even when faith feels small, it's still enough to move mountains.

Glow-Up Challenge: When doubt creeps in today, whisper, "I still believe," and let that be your act of faith.

Glow Through the Storm

Day 150
Stand Firm in the Wind

May 30

"After you have done everything, to stand."
Ephesians 6:13

Sometimes the most powerful thing you can do is simply stay standing. The enemy wants you to crumble. God just wants you to stand still and stay sure.

Affirmation: I stand firm. Clothed in faith and fortified by grace.

Glow-Up Challenge: Pause today and reflect on everything you've already overcome. Your resilience is proof of God's power.

Glow Through the Storm

Day 151
God's Got This

May 31

"You will not have to fight this battle. Take up your positions; stand firm and see the deliverance the LORD will give you."
2 Chronicles 20:17

You don't have to handle everything. Some battles belong entirely to God. The moment you surrender, Heaven steps in.

Affirmation: I let go of control and trust that God is fighting for me.

Glow-Up Challenge: Write down one thing that's been heavy on your heart. Then release it to God in prayer, fully.

Glow Through the Storm

Day 152
The Glow of Gratitude

June 1

"Give thanks to the LORD, for he is good; his love endures forever."
Psalm 118:11

Gratitude is the flashlight that cuts through any darkness. The more thankful you are, the more light you see.

Affirmation: Gratitude keeps my glow alive, even in gray skies.

Glow-Up Challenge: List five things you're thankful for in the middle of your current storm. Watch how your mood shifts.

Glow Through the Storm

Day 153
Storm-Proof Peace

June 2

"May the Lord of peace Himself, give you peace at all times and in every way."
2 Thessalonians 3:16

Peace isn't fragile. It's fortified by faith. When you let God rule your heart, chaos can swirl around you but never inside you.

Affirmation: My peace is anchored in Christ. No wind can shake it loose.

Glow-Up Challenge: Do one grounding practice today deep breathing, prayer, or stillness to re-center your peace.

Glow Through the Storm

Day 154
Beauty Beyond the Battle

June 3

"After you have suffered a little while, the God of all grace will Himself restore you and make you strong."
1 Peter 5:10

Every storm's aftermath reveals transformation. Your scars are not shame. They're proof that grace was greater.

Affirmation: I wear beauty where there once were ashes. I am proof of restoration.

Glow-Up Challenge: Reflect on one "battle scar" and how it shaped your compassion or wisdom.

Glow Through the Storm

Day 155
Radiant Resilience

June 4

*"We are hard pressed on every side, but not crushed...
struck down, but not destroyed."*
2 Corinthians 4:8–9

Resilience is your divine glow-up armor. You've faced storms and still sparkle. You don't shine despite what you've been through. You shine because of it.

Affirmation: My resilience is radiant. I glow through every storm with God beside me.

Glow-Up Challenge: Speak this aloud: "I am still standing, still shining, and still chosen."

Glow Through the Storm

Day 156
Peace Over Panic

June 5

"Do not let your hearts be troubled. You believe in God; believe also in Me."
John 14:1

Panic is loud, but peace is louder when you let faith lead. Every storm has a sound. Choose to tune your heart to God's calm voice instead of fear's noise.

Affirmation: I choose peace over panic. My faith silences fear.

Glow-Up Challenge: When anxiety rises today, take one deep breath and repeat: "God, You are my calm."

Glow Through the Storm

Day 157
Purpose in Pressure

June 6

"We rejoice in our sufferings, because we know that suffering produces perseverance; perseverance, character; and character, hope."
Romans 5:3–4

Pressure doesn't break you. It builds you. God uses tight places to shape solid faith. Diamonds form in darkness, and so does destiny.

Affirmation: Pressure produces purpose. I'm being refined, not reduced.

Glow-Up Challenge: Write about one situation where pressure led to personal growth or greater clarity.

Glow Through the Storm

Day 158
Keep Walking

June 7

"The Lord makes firm the steps of the one who delights in Him; though they stumble, they will not fall."
Psalm 37:23–24

The secret to glowing through storms? Keep walking. One faithful step at a time. Healing, progress, and breakthrough all happen in motion.

Affirmation: Even when the path is unclear, I keep walking by faith.

Glow-Up Challenge: Take an intentional walk today. Let every step remind you that forward is still forward.

Glow Through the Storm

Day 159
When the Clouds Clear

June 8

"Weeping may stay for the night, but rejoicing comes in the morning."
Psalm 30:5

Every storm has an expiration date. When the clouds finally part, what remains is clarity. A renewed view of God's faithfulness and your own strength.

Affirmation: The night has passed. Joy is rising with the morning light.

Glow-Up Challenge: Write a "morning prayer" of gratitude for what's starting to clear in your life.

Glow Through the Storm

Day 160
Glow Through Grace

June 9

"For it is by grace you have been saved, through faith."
Ephesians 2:8

Grace is what keeps your glow steady. It carries you when effort fades. Healing may have strengthened you, but grace sustains you through the storms.

Affirmation: Grace covers me, fuels me, and glows through me.

Glow-Up Challenge: Speak grace over yourself today. Replace every "I should've" with "I'm still growing."

Glow Through the Storm

Day 161
The Power of Persevering Praise

June 10

"Enter His gates with thanksgiving and His courts with praise."
Psalm 100:4

Praise is your storm strategy. It opens the door for peace to enter and anxiety to leave. Worship reminds your heart who's in charge of the weather.

Affirmation: My praise is louder than my problems. Joy is my response to pressure.

Glow-Up Challenge: Turn your next complaint into praise. Say, "God, thank You for working even in this."

Glow Through the Storm

Day 162
Strength Restored

June 11

"He satisfies your desires with good things so that your youth is renewed like the eagle's."
Psalm 103:5

You've been grounded for a reason: to grow new wings. Strength is returning, and the storm has taught you how to soar higher than before.

Affirmation: My strength is renewed. I rise higher through every storm.

Glow-Up Challenge: Write down one area of your life that's been renewed or restored through challenge. Thank God for your wings.

Glow Through the Storm

Day 163
Rising After the Rain

June 12

"Though I have fallen, I will rise. Though I sit in darkness, the Lord will be my light."
Micah 7:8

The rain may have soaked your spirit, but it never drowned your faith. Rising after the storm is proof that what fell apart couldn't destroy what was rooted.

Affirmation: I rise stronger after every storm. God's light lifts me higher.

Glow-Up Challenge: Write a short victory statement about what you've overcome. Read it aloud as a declaration of strength.

Glow Through the Storm

Day 164
The Gift of Resilience

June 13

"In all these things we are more than conquerors through Him who loved us."
Romans 8:37

Resilience is grace in motion. It's your spirit's ability to recover faster each time because you've learned where your strength comes from.

Affirmation: I am more than a conqueror. I am resilient through God's love.

Glow-Up Challenge: List three moments where you bounced back when you thought you couldn't.

Glow Through the Storm

Day 165
Faith That Finishes

June 14

"I have fought the good fight, I have finished the race, I have kept the faith."
2 Timothy 4:7

It's not how fast you ran, but how faithfully you stayed the course. Finishing strong means trusting that every step, even the slow ones, mattered.

Affirmation: I finish what faith started in me.

Glow-Up Challenge: Reflect on something you completed recently. Thank God for the grace to see it through.

Glow Through the Storm

Day 166
The Beauty of Becoming Unbreakable

June 15

"He alone is my rock and my salvation; I will not be shaken."
Psalm 62:6

Unbreakable doesn't mean untouched. It means unshaken by life's weight. You're stronger now because you've learned to lean, not just stand.

Affirmation: I am unbreakable because my strength is built on the Rock.

Glow-Up Challenge: Pray this short prayer: "Lord, thank You that my strength is not my own. It's Yours."

Glow Through the Storm

Day 167
Lessons in the Lightning

June 16

"He reveals the deep things of darkness and brings utter darkness into the light."
Job 12:22

Even lightning teaches. It reveals what's been hidden. The bright flashes in life's storms often bring the deepest revelation.

⚜

Affirmation: Every flash of trial brings a spark of wisdom.

Glow-Up Challenge: Write down one thing the storm has revealed to you about God, yourself, or others.

Glow Through the Storm

Day 168
The Peace After the Pour

June 17

"You will keep in perfect peace those minds are steadfast, because they trust in you."
Isaiah 26:3

After the rain comes rest. The kind of peace you can't explain, only experience. This peace isn't the absence of problems. It's the evidence of Presence.

Affirmation: I rest in peace that passes understanding. God guards my heart and mind.

Glow-Up Challenge: Spend ten minutes in quiet gratitude today. No requests, just peace.

Glow Through the Storm

Day 169
Glow in the Aftermath

June 18

"Those who sow with tears will reap with songs of joy."
Psalm 126:5

Every storm plants seeds. The tears you cried were watering your next season's joy. This is your after-glow: radiant, restored, and resilient.

Affirmation: I am glowing in my aftermath. Joy has replaced my tears.

Glow-Up Challenge: Write a short praise note or gratitude prayer. Title it "My Afterglow."

Phase 3
Reflection
Glowing Through the Storm

Take a slow, deep breath. You made it through.

This was the phase that tested your light, and you didn't just survive. You shined. Every tear watered your wisdom. Every challenge became a testimony. Every storm revealed a steadier faith within you.

You've learned that peace isn't found in perfect days, but in a perfect Savior. You've discovered that the same God who calms storms also walks with you through them. You've proven that your glow doesn't fade in the rain. It reflects the Light of the One who never leaves.

This is what divine resilience looks like. It is radiant faith forged in the wind and made stronger by grace.

Glow Through the Storm

Journal Prompts

What has this storm season revealed about God's character?

How has my view of strength or success shifted since learning to "glow through"?

What battles did I overcome that I once thought would break me?

What does peace look and feel like for me now?

Glow Through the Storm

Prayer

Lord, thank You for being my calm within every storm.
You steadied my spirit, stretched my faith, and strengthened my roots.
Help me carry this peace into every new challenge, knowing You are my shelter and my song.
Let my light reflect Your faithfulness wherever I go. Amen.

Affirmation

I glow through every storm because my peace is anchored in God's power, not my circumstances.

Phase 4

Radiant Faith

The rain has passed, and the light is breaking through the clouds. Now begins a new chapter. One not built on survival, but on shining boldly.

Phase 4 is all about Radiant Faith. It is about walking with divine confidence, trusting boldly, and living as the light of Christ in a world that needs hope.

This phase teaches that faith isn't just belief. It's brilliance. It's courage clothed in grace. It's walking so closely with God that even your presence carries peace.

You've been rooted, healed, and refined. Now, it's time to radiate.

Radiant Faith

Day 170
Faith That Radiates

June 19

"Let your light shine before others, that they may see your good deeds and glorify your Father in heaven."
Matthew 5:16

Faith isn't meant to stay hidden. It's meant to glow. When you live boldly for God, your life becomes a walking reflection of His goodness.

Affirmation: My faith shines brightly. I am a reflection of God's light.

Glow-Up Challenge: Do one thing today that shares God's love. A word, an act, or even a smile.

Radiant Faith

Day 171
Confidence in Christ

June 20

"So do not throw away your confidence; it will be richly rewarded."
Hebrews 10:35

Confidence isn't pride. It's peace in knowing who walks beside you. Radiant faith comes from remembering that God already equipped you for the path you're on.

Affirmation: I walk with divine confidence. I am fully equipped for my purpose.

Glow-Up Challenge: Write down one area of your life where you need holy confidence, then declare: "God's got me here."

Radiant Faith

Day 172
Bold Belief

June 21

"Whatever you ask for in prayer, believe that you have received it, and it will be yours."
Mark 11:24

Faith shines brightest when it believes boldly. God doesn't want timid prayers. He wants trust-filled expectation. Speak it, believe it, and watch it bloom.

Affirmation: I believe boldly and expect miracles with confident faith.

Glow-Up Challenge: Pray boldly today for what only God can accomplish.

Radiant Faith

Day 173
The Glow of Gratitude

June 22

"Let the peace of Christ rule in your hearts, since as members of one body you were called to peace. And be thankful."
Colossians 3:15

Gratitude is radiant. When you are thankful, your energy shifts and your spirit glows. Gratitude magnifies blessings and turns ordinary days into miracles.

Affirmation: My gratitude is contagious. I radiate joy wherever I go.

Glow-Up Challenge: Thank God for five things you once prayed for. Celebrate how far you've come.

Radiant Faith

Day 174
Unshakable Trust

June 23

"You will keep in perfect peace those whose minds are steadfast, because they trust in You."
Isaiah 26:3

Radiant faith means trusting even when you can't trace the plan. When you walk with unshakable trust, peace follows your every step.

Affirmation: My trust in God is my strength and my stability.

Glow-Up Challenge: Surrender one lingering worry, out loud, and replace it with the words, "I trust You completely."

Radiant Faith

Day 175
Overflowing Joy

June 24

"I have told you this so that My joy may be in you and that your joy may be complete."
John 15:11

Joy is the evidence of radiant faith. It's not forced. It's felt. When you walk closely with God, joy flows naturally, even in ordinary moments.

Affirmation: My joy overflows from God's presence within me.

Glow-Up Challenge: Do something today purely because it brings you joy. Your laughter is praise in motion.

Radiant Faith

Day 176
Glowing with Purpose

June 25

"For we are God's masterpiece, created in Christ Jesus to do good works."
Ephesians 2:10

You were designed with divine purpose. Your purpose is to let your light shine. Radiant faith means showing up boldly in your calling, knowing your life is an answered prayer for someone else.

Affirmation: I am God's masterpiece. I am shining through my purpose with passion and peace.

Glow-Up Challenge: Take one small action today toward something that aligns with your calling. Trust that it matters.

Radiant Faith

Day 177
Faith Over Feelings

June 26

"For we walk by faith, not by sight."
2 Corinthians 5:7

Faith doesn't wait to feel ready. It moves because it knows Who's leading. Feelings fluctuate, but faith stands firm on truth.

Affirmation: I am guided by faith, not my emotions.

Glow-Up Challenge: When your feelings try to lead today, pause and ask, "What does faith say instead?"

Radiant Faith

Day 178
Radiance in Rejection

June 27

"If the world hates you, keep in mind that it hated Me first."
John 15:18

Not everyone will understand your glow. That's okay. Rejection often means you're walking in divine direction. Let God's approval matter most.

Affirmation: I am secure in God's love. Rejection only refines my purpose.

Glow-Up Challenge: Reflect on a time rejection redirected you toward something better. Write down how God used it for good.

Radiant Faith

Day 179
Faith That Speaks Life

June 28

"The tongue has the power of life and death."
Proverbs 18:21

Radiant faith speaks victory even before it sees it. Your words can either dim your light or fuel your fire. Choose to speak faith into every situation.

Affirmation: My words carry light. I speak life over myself and others.

Glow-Up Challenge: Catch one negative phrase you'd normally say and replace it with a declaration of faith.

Radiant Faith

Day 180
Courage to Step Out

June 29

"Be strong and courageous. Do not be afraid; do not be discouraged, for the Lord your God will be with you wherever you go."
Joshua 1:9

Faith gets brighter with movement. God can't steer a parked heart. Take the step, even if it's small. Courage is obedience in action.

Affirmation: I walk boldly into every calling with God's strength beside me.

Glow-Up Challenge: Take one brave step today towards something you've been delaying, and trust God to meet you there.

Radiant Faith

Day 181
Radiant Resilience

June 30

"They will have no fear of bad news; their hearts are steadfast, trusting in the Lord."
Psalm 112:7

Faith doesn't fear the unknown because it already knows the ending. God wins. Radiant resilience means staying calm even when outcomes are uncertain.

Affirmation: My faith is steady. My heart stays peaceful through uncertainty.

Glow-Up Challenge: When fear arises, take one minute to breathe and say, "God, I trust You with what I can't control."

Radiant Faith

Day 182
The Power of Faith-Filled Friendships

July 1

"Two are better than one… if either falls, one can help the other up."
Ecclesiastes 4:9–10

Faith grows faster in community. God didn't design you to glow alone. Your sisters in Christ are mirrors that reflect His love back to you.

Affirmation: I am surrounded by faith-filled friends who help me shine brighter.

Glow-Up Challenge: Reach out to one friend today and remind her how much she's strengthened your faith.

Radiant Faith

Day 183
The Glow of Grace

July 2

"Grow in the grace and knowledge of our Lord and Savior Jesus Christ."
2 Peter 3:18

Faith and grace are divine dance partners. Grace fuels your faith, and faith magnifies grace. The more you receive both, the lighter your spirit becomes.

Affirmation: I grow in grace daily. My faith shines brighter through God's mercy.

Glow-Up Challenge: When you feel pressure to be perfect today, pause and whisper, "Grace over grind."

Radiant Faith

Day 184
Faith That Moves Mountains

July 3

"If you have faith as small as a mustard seed... nothing will be impossible for you."
Matthew 17:20

Radiant faith doesn't need to be big. It just needs to be real. Even the smallest seed of belief can move the mountains in your path.

Affirmation: My faith may be small, but it's mighty because it's rooted in God.

Glow-Up Challenge: Speak to one "mountain" in your life today. Declare that it must move in Jesus' name.

Radiant Faith

Day 185
When Faith Feels Fierce

July 4

Take up the shield of faith, with which you can extinguish all the flaming arrows of the evil one."
Ephesians 6:16

Some days, faith is fire. Protective, powerful, and bold. It's what shields your peace when doubt tries to creep in.

Affirmation: My faith is my armor. Nothing can dim the fire God placed within me.

Glow-Up Challenge: When negativity appears today, visualize your shield of faith rising to protect your spirit.

Radiant Faith

Day 186
Rooted in Revelation

July 5

"Your word is a lamp for my feet, a light on my path."
Psalm 119:105

Radiant faith grows from revelation. When you read God's Word, your spirit absorbs truth that lights the way forward.

Affirmation: God's Word guides my glow. His truth keeps me steady.

Glow-Up Challenge: Read one Psalm or Proverb today and write down the verse that speaks to your current season.

Radiant Faith

Day 187
Overflowing Faith

July 6

"May the God of hope fill you with all joy and peace as you trust in Him, so that you may overflow with hope."
Romans 15:13

Faith is meant to overflow, to pour out as peace, joy, and compassion. The more you trust, the more your presence becomes healing to others.

Affirmation: My faith overflows with hope and light for others.

Glow-Up Challenge: Encourage someone today with a reminder that hope still lives. You might be the overflow they need.

Radiant Faith

Day 188
Fearless Faith

July 7

"For God has not given us a spirit of fear, but of power, love, and a sound mind."
2 Timothy 1:7

Fear dims. Faith ignites. Radiant faith replaces panic with power and worry with wisdom. Fear has no authority over the one who knows who she is in Christ.

Affirmation: I walk in power, love, and divine peace. Fear has no hold on me.

Glow-Up Challenge: When fear speaks today, answer back with Scripture, out loud.

Radiant Faith

Day 189
Faith That Flourishes

July 8

"Blessed is the one who trusts in the Lord... they will be like a tree planted by the water."
Jeremiah 17:7–8

Faith doesn't just survive. It flourishes. Even in dry seasons, your roots reach living water. Flourishing faith doesn't fade with time. It deepens with trust.

Affirmation: I flourish in faith. My roots reach divine strength daily.

Glow-Up Challenge: Water your spirit today read, pray, or worship and thank God for the growth you can't yet see.

Radiant Faith

Day 190
Glowing in His Glory

July 9

"The earth will be filled with the knowledge of the glory of the Lord as the waters cover the sea."
Habakkuk 2:14

When your faith shines, you reflect His glory. You become part of the promise that His light will fill the earth through those who love Him boldly.

Affirmation: I glow with God's glory. My life is a reflection of His light.

Glow-Up Challenge: Thank God for trusting you to carry His light, and pray that your glow continues to draw others to Him.

Radiant Faith

Day 191
Faith That Glows Boldly

July 10

"Arise, shine, for your light has come, and the glory of the Lord rises upon you."
Isaiah 60:1

You were never meant to shrink your shine. Radiant faith steps forward boldly, knowing that your light doesn't compete. It completes God's picture of grace on earth.

Affirmation: I rise in bold faith. My glow blesses others.

Glow-Up Challenge: Step into something today that once intimidated you, and do it confidently, knowing you're clothed in His light.

Radiant Faith

Day 192
Walking in Wisdom

July 11

"Blessed are those who find wisdom, those who gain understanding."
Proverbs 3:13

Faith isn't blind. It's insightful. Godly wisdom keeps your glow balanced between discernment and devotion. Faith walks bravely, but wisdom walks mindfully.

Affirmation: My faith is guided by wisdom. I move with clarity and grace.

Glow-Up Challenge: Ask God for wisdom before making a decision today, then listen quietly for His peace.

Radiant Faith

Day 193
Faith That Inspires

July 12

"The Lord's message rang out from you… your faith in God has become known everywhere."
1 Thessalonians 1:8

Your glow speaks louder than your words. People notice peace that doesn't fade and joy that doesn't depend on circumstance. Let your life preach hope without even trying.

Affirmation: My faith is contagious. My glow inspires others toward God.

Glow-Up Challenge: Post or share one encouraging truth today. Something that uplifts others from your own testimony.

Radiant Faith

Day 194
Anchored in Identity

July 13

"You are a chosen people, a royal priesthood, a holy nation, God's special possession."
1 Peter 2:9

Your glow comes from knowing who you are and whose you are. Identity in Christ frees you from seeking validation. You're already chosen, already enough.

Affirmation: I am chosen, cherished, and complete in Christ.

Glow-Up Challenge: Write "I am chosen" somewhere visible a mirror, planner, or phone as your daily reminder.

Radiant Faith

Day 195
The Strength of Still Faith

July 14

"The LORD your God, who is going before you, will fight for you."
Deuteronomy 1:30

Faith doesn't always roar. Sometimes it rests. Still faith trusts God's unseen movement more than visible results.

Affirmation: My stillness is a sign of trust, not weakness.

Glow-Up Challenge: Practice five minutes of total quiet. No music, no lists, just rest in awareness of God's presence.

Radiant Faith

Day 196
Radiant Influence

July 15

"Then you will shine among them like stars in the sky."
Philippians 2:15

When you walk in radiant faith, you change atmospheres. You don't have to force influence. Your light naturally leads others home to God.

Affirmation: I am a light in every room. My presence carries God's peace.

Glow-Up Challenge: Bring calm or kindness into one space today. Your glow will do more than words ever could.

Radiant Faith

Day 197
Faith That Finishes Strong

July 16

"Let us run with perseverance the race marked out for us, fixing our eyes on Jesus."
Hebrews 12:1–2

Faith doesn't fizzle. It finishes. Radiant faith keeps running even when it's tired, because it knows who waits at the finish line.

Affirmation: I finish strong, focused, and full of faith.

Glow-Up Challenge: Reflect on one area of your life that's nearing completion. Thank God for the endurance to finish well.

Radiant Faith

Day 198
Faith That Multiplies

July 17

"Give, and it will be given to you… a good measure, pressed down, shaken together and running over."
Luke 6:38

Faith grows when you pour it out. The more you give love, hope, encouragement , the more God multiplies it back to you.

Affirmation: My faith overflows. I live in divine abundance.

Glow-Up Challenge: Offer one act of generosity today. Give joyfully and trust God to multiply it.

Radiant Faith

Day 199
Faith in the Fire

July 18

"Look! I see four men walking around in the fire... and the fourth looks like a son of the gods."
Daniel 3:25

The fire doesn't destroy your faith. It displays it. When you walk through flames with God, the heat becomes holy.

Affirmation: I walk through fire with grace. God is with me in every test.

Glow-Up Challenge: Reflect on a "fire" you've faced. How did God show up in unexpected ways?

Radiant Faith

Day 200
Faith That Forgives

July 19

"Be kind and compassionate to one another, forgiving each other, just as Christ forgave you."
Ephesians 4:23

Forgiveness isn't a weakness. It's strength in surrender. Radiant faith forgives freely, because it trusts God with justice and healing.

Affirmation: I release bitterness and radiate freedom through forgiveness.

Glow-Up Challenge: Write the name of someone you need to forgive, and pray for peace over both of your hearts.

Radiant Faith

Day 201
Faith That Builds Bridges

July 20

"If it is possible, as far as it depends on you, live at peace with everyone."
Romans 12:18

Faith connects, not divides. It's easy to build walls. Radiant faith builds bridges. Love becomes the light that crosses differences and heals divides.

Affirmation: I am a peacemaker. My presence creates connection and healing.

Glow-Up Challenge: Reach out to someone you've drifted from. Offer grace, not explanation.

Radiant Faith

Day 202
Unapologetic Faith

July 21

"For I am not ashamed of the gospel, because it is the power of God that brings salvation."
Romans 1:16

Radiant faith stands tall, unashamed and unafraid. You don't have to dim your light to fit in. It was meant to stand out and illuminate.

Affirmation: I am unashamed of my faith. My light belongs on display.

Glow-Up Challenge: Share your faith story, even a small part, with someone today.

Radiant Faith

Day 203
The Glow of Gratitude Revisited

July 22

"Give thanks to the Lord, for He is good; His love endures forever."
1 Chronicles 16:34

Every season deserves thanks. The highs, the lows, and the in-betweens. Gratitude keeps your glow pure and your heart aligned with heaven.

Affirmation: I overflow with gratitude. Every breath is a thank You to God.

Glow-Up Challenge: Start a gratitude list for this week. Add one new blessing each day.

Radiant Faith

Day 204
Faith That Bears Fruit

July 23

"But the fruit of the Spirit is love, joy, peace, forbearance, kindness, goodness, faithfulness, gentleness and self-control. Against such things there is no law."
Galatians 5:22-23

Radiant faith produces visible change: peace, patience, kindness, and joy. The glow within you nourishes the world around you.

Affirmation: I stay rooted in Christ and flourish with lasting fruit.

Glow-Up Challenge: Reflect on one "fruit" of your faith, something in your life that has grown because you stayed connected to God.

Radiant Faith

Day 205
Faith That Overflows with Love

July 24

"And now these three remain: faith, hope and love. But the greatest of these is love."
1 Corinthians 13:13

Love is the purest proof of faith. When your heart glows with compassion, forgiveness, and grace, you're living your strongest testimony.

Affirmation: My faith expresses itself through love in every interaction.

Glow-Up Challenge: Go out of your way to show love today, through words, presence, or prayer.

Radiant Faith

Day 206
Unmovable Faith

July 25

"Those who trust in the Lord are like Mount Zion, which cannot be shaken but endures forever."
Psalm 125:1

Radiant faith doesn't crumble under pressure. When storms shake the world, you remain grounded, not because of your strength, but because of your Source.

Affirmation: My faith is unmovable, rooted in the everlasting strength of God.

Glow-Up Challenge: Each time you feel shaken today, whisper: "My faith stands firm."

Radiant Faith

Day 207
Faith That Reflects Peace

July 26

"Whatever you have learned or received or heard from me, put it into practice. And the God of peace will be with you."
Philippians 4:9

True faith reflects peace, not panic. When you live out what you've learned, your spirit becomes a mirror of heaven's calm.

Affirmation: I am a vessel of peace. My faith brings calm wherever I go.

Glow-Up Challenge: Practice being the calm in one situation that feels tense or chaotic today.

Radiant Faith

Day 208
Radiant Faith in Action

July 27

"Faith by itself, if it is not accompanied by action, is dead."
James 2:17

Faith glows when it's lived. It's not about what you say you believe, but how you walk, serve, and love through it daily.

Affirmation: My faith is alive, active, and visible in all I do.

Glow-Up Challenge: Take one faith-fueled action today. Something that shows love in motion.

Radiant Faith

Day 209
Faith That Overcomes Fear

July 28

"There is no fear in love. But perfect love drives out fear."
1 John 4:18

Radiant faith is fearless because it's full of love. The closer you walk with God, the less room fear has to whisper.

Affirmation: Love fills me so completely that fear can't stay.

Glow-Up Challenge: When fear tries to rise, say out loud: "Love lives here. Fear does not."

Radiant Faith

Day 210
Faith That Lifts Others

July 29

"Carry each other's burdens, and in this way you will fulfill the law of Christ."
Galatians 6:2

Faith isn't just personal. It's communal. Radiant believers lift others through prayer, presence, and encouragement.

Affirmation: My faith uplifts others. I am a light that helps hearts rise.

Glow-Up Challenge: Pray intentionally for someone else today, and if you can, let them know they're covered.

Radiant Faith

Day 211
Living Light

July 30

"I am the light of the world. Whoever follows Me will never walk in darkness, but will have the light of life."
John 8:12

When you walk with Jesus, you don't just reflect light. You become it. Radiant faith means carrying His presence everywhere you go, so darkness has no hold.

Affirmation: I walk in the light of Christ. My life is a living glow of grace.

Glow-Up Challenge: End your day by lighting a candle and thanking God for being the source of your everlasting light.

Radiant Faith

Day 212
Faith That Flows

July 31

"Whoever believes in Me, as Scripture has said, rivers of living water will flow from within them."
John 7:38

Radiant faith is not stagnant. It's a steady flow of life, peace, and love. When you stay connected to the Source, you naturally refresh everyone around you.

Affirmation: Living water flows through me. I refresh others with God's love.

Glow-Up Challenge: Do something today that pours life into someone else, whether it's a kind word, a prayer, or a listening ear.

Radiant Faith

Day 213
Unwavering Faith

August 1

"When you ask, you must believe and not doubt."
James 1:6

Unwavering faith trusts without hesitation. It doesn't go back and forth between fear and faith. It decides once, and stands firm in that belief.

Affirmation: My heart is steady. I trust God completely and without wavering.

Glow-Up Challenge: Each time you're tempted to doubt today, say: "Faith wins."

Radiant Faith

Day 214
Faith That Restores

August 2

"He restores my soul; He guides me along the right paths for His name's sake."
Psalm 23:3

Radiant faith doesn't just shine. It restores. When your soul is tired, God's light gently revives you, reminding you that rest is part of faith too.

Affirmation: My soul is restored daily by the peace of God's presence.

Glow-Up Challenge: Rest intentionally today. Even five quiet minutes count. Let restoration be your act of faith.

Radiant Faith

Day 215
Faith That Celebrates

August 3

"Rejoice in the Lord always. I will say it again: Rejoice!"
Philippians 4:4

Joy is a declaration of faith. Radiant believers don't wait for everything to be perfect to celebrate. They rejoice because they know Who holds the outcome.

Affirmation: My joy is my praise. Celebration keeps my spirit bright.

Glow-Up Challenge: Celebrate something small today: your progress, your peace, or your perseverance.

Radiant Faith

Day 216
Faith That Impacts Generations

August 4

"Know therefore that the Lord your God is God; He is the faithful God, keeping His covenant of love to a thousand generations."
Deuteronomy 7:9

Your faith doesn't end with you. It echoes through generations. Every prayer you pray and seed you sow plants legacy in the soil of eternity.

Affirmation: My faith is generational. I'm planting seeds that will outlive me.

Glow-Up Challenge: Pray a blessing over your family line. For faith, healing, and favor to flow forward.

Radiant Faith

Day 217
Faith That Radiates Peace

August 5

"You will keep in perfect peace those whose minds are steadfast, because they trust in You."
Isaiah 26:3

When your faith is unwavering, peace becomes permanent. Radiant peace is not momentary. It's the byproduct of continual trust.

Affirmation: My mind is steady, my heart is calm, and my faith is rooted in peace.

Glow-Up Challenge: Take a "peace pause" today. It can look like a deep breath and a whispered prayer of thanks for the calm within.

Radiant Faith

Day 218
Unstoppable Faith

August 6

"If God is for us, who can be against us?"
Romans 8:31

This is the glow that can't be dimmed. Unstoppable faith moves with divine confidence, knowing that nothing not fear, failure, or opposition can stop God's plan.

Affirmation: I am unstoppable in faith. God's favor clears my path.

Glow-Up Challenge: End your day by declaring aloud: "Nothing can stop what God has started in me."

Radiant Faith

Phase 4
Reflection
Radiant Faith

Take a deep breath, beautiful soul.
You've reached the light-filled heart of your glow-up. The place where your faith no longer flickers. It burns steady.

This phase wasn't just about believing. It was about becoming. You learned to walk boldly, to trust deeply, and to radiate peace without trying. You've discovered that faith isn't something you wear on good days. It's who you are, every day.

The glow you carry now is not surface-deep. It's sacred. It's faith that moves, breathes, and transforms. You've become living light, a reflection of the One who called you out of darkness and into His marvelous grace.

Let this be your holy reminder: Your radiance was never meant to end here. It's meant to restore the world around you.

Radiant Faith

Journal Prompts

How has my faith grown stronger, steadier, or more joyful during this phase?

In what ways has my light touched others around me?

What does "radiant faith" mean to me now, and how can I live it daily?

What habits, prayers, or mindsets have helped me stay anchored in trust?

Radiant Faith

Prayer

Lord, thank You for making my faith radiant.
You've taught me to stand firm in storms, to walk boldly in peace,
and to glow with Your glory wherever I go.
Let my faith continue to shine as a beacon for others who need hope.
Keep my heart humble, my trust unshaken, and my spirit forever
lit with Your love. Amen.

Affirmation

My faith radiates peace, power, and purpose. I am a living
reflection of God's glory.

Phase 5

Restored to Shine

This is it. The home stretch of your Holy Glow-Up.
You've been rooted, healed, refined, and made radiant. Now it's time to rise restored, whole, empowered, and shining from the inside out.

Phase 5: Restored to Shine is where your full transformation unfolds. It's not about starting over. It's about walking in divine renewal. You'll celebrate restoration in every area: body, mind, spirit, relationships, and purpose.

This final phase is your spiritual glow-up realized. Not perfection, but peace. Not striving, but shining. You're no longer becoming. You are.

So take a breath, lift your chin, and step boldly into your restored glow. It's your time to shine.

Restored to Shine

Day 219
Fully Restored

August 7

"I will restore to you the years that the locusts have eaten."
Joel 2:25

God wastes nothing, not even your hardest seasons. What was lost, delayed, or broken is being restored in ways more beautiful than before.

Affirmation: God is restoring everything I thought was gone in His timing, His way, and His glory.

Glow-Up Challenge: Write a list of what God has restored in your life. Relationships, peace, health, or hope.

Restored to Shine

Day 220
Beauty in the Bloom

August 8

"He will give a crown of beauty for ashes."
Isaiah 61:3

Restoration is when what once burned now blossoms. Every scar becomes sacred proof that God transforms pain into purpose.

Affirmation: I wear beauty where ashes once were. I bloom with grace and gratitude.

Glow-Up Challenge: Reflect on one past hardship that produced unexpected beauty.

Restored to Shine

Day 221
Restored in Strength

August 9

"It is God who arms me with strength and keeps my way secure."
Psalm 18:32

You're not just healed. You're fortified. Restoration means your strength is no longer your own. It's sustained by divine power.

Affirmation: My strength is restored and anchored in divine power.

Glow-Up Challenge: Do something today that makes you feel strong spiritually, emotionally, or physically.

Restored to Shine

Day 222
Wholeness Within

August 10

"You are complete in Him."
Colossians 2:10

Restoration brings peace because it ends striving. You no longer need to search outside yourself for validation. God already made you whole.

Affirmation: I am whole, healed, and complete in Christ.

Glow-Up Challenge: Write a love letter to yourself from God's perspective. Make sure it is full of grace and truth.

Restored to Shine

Day 223
Overflowing Blessings

August 11

"My cup overflows."
Psalm 23:5

When God restores, He doesn't just refill. He overflows. Restoration means abundance. Joy, opportunity, and favor beyond what you imagined.

Affirmation: My cup overflows. I walk in divine abundance and peace.

Glow-Up Challenge: Share one of your blessings today. It can be a gift, encouragement, or testimony that lifts another's spirit.

Restored to Shine

Day 224
The Glow of Gratitude

August 12

"Devote yourselves to prayer, being watchful and thankful."
Colossians 4:2

Gratitude is the finishing touch of restoration. When you give thanks, you seal your healing with joy.

Affirmation: Gratitude keeps my glow radiant and my heart at rest.

Glow-Up Challenge: Write a "restoration gratitude list" that includes ten things you thank God for in this season.

Day 225
Restored to Shine

August 13

"Arise, shine, for your light has come, and the glory of the Lord rises upon you."
Isaiah 60:1

This is your glow-up realized. You are walking proof of redemption, healed, renewed, and radiant with His glory. You shine not to be seen, but to show the world what grace can do.

Affirmation: I am restored to shine. Radiant, renewed, and rooted in divine purpose.

Glow-Up Challenge: Do one bold thing today that honors your glow. Share your story, your faith, or your joy.

Restored to Shine

Day 226
Rest in Renewal

August 14

"He gives power to the weak and strength to the powerless."
Isaiah 40:29

True restoration isn't about doing more. It's about being renewed in stillness. You don't have to chase what God freely gives through rest.

Affirmation: Rest restores me. I am strengthened in God's stillness.

Glow-Up Challenge: Take time today to pause, breathe, and do nothing but be present with God.

Restored to Shine

Day 227
The Glow of Alignment

August 15

"In their hearts humans plan their course, but the Lord establishes their steps."
Proverbs 16:9

Restoration aligns your path with divine timing. When your steps match His rhythm, you walk in ease instead of effort.

Affirmation: I am aligned with divine purpose. Peace leads my path.

Glow-Up Challenge: Surrender one plan to God today. Ask Him to align it with His perfect will.

Restored to Shine

Day 228
Restored Perspective

August 16

"You intended to harm me, but God intended it for good to accomplish what is now being done, the saving of many lives."
Genesis 50:20

Looking back through healed eyes reveals that even the hard things had holy purpose. Restoration changes how you see more than what you've seen.

Affirmation: I see my past through grace and my future through faith.

Glow-Up Challenge: Reflect on one past challenge. Identify how God used it to shape your strength or compassion.

Restored to Shine

Day 229
Peace That Glows

August 17

"Therefore, since we have been justified through faith, we have eace with God through our Lord Jesus Christ."
Romans 5:1

Peace is the perfume of restoration. It lingers long after the chaos ends. You no longer need to chase peace. You carry it.

Affirmation: Peace surrounds me, fills me, and flows through me.

Glow-Up Challenge: Practice carrying peace today. Respond gently, move slowly, and speak kindly.

Restored to Shine

Day 230
Restored Confidence

August 18

"We constantly pray for you, that our God may make you worthy of his calling, and that by his power he may bring to fruition your every desire for goodness."
2 Thessalonians 1:1

Confidence in restoration comes from knowing the story isn't over. God finishes every work He starts, including you.

Affirmation: I walk in restored confidence. Trusting God's perfect completion.

Glow-Up Challenge: List three things you've grown in this year spiritually, emotionally, or personally and thank God for each.

Restored to Shine

Day 231
Radiant Relationships

August 19

"Be completely humble and gentle; be patient, bearing with one another in love."
Ephesians 4:2–3

Restoration extends into your relationships. When your heart is healed, your connections reflect it. Grace replaces judgment, patience replaces pressure.

Affirmation: I nurture relationships with grace, patience, and love.

Glow-Up Challenge: Reach out to someone meaningful in your life. Tell them what you appreciate about them.

Restored to Shine

Day 232
Restored Joy

August 20

"Restore to me the joy of Your salvation."
Psalm 51:12

Joy is the crown of restoration. It's not circumstantial. It's sacred. This joy is your strength, your song, and your glow reborn.

❀

Affirmation: My joy is restored and radiant. It flows from divine renewal.

Glow-Up Challenge: Do one thing today that fills you with joy and laughter, and thank God for your restored spirit.

Restored to Shine

Day 233
Faithful in the Flow

August 21

"My times are in your hands."
Psalm 31:15

Restoration teaches you to stop forcing and start flowing. God's timing is never late. It's always layered with beauty you can't yet see.

Affirmation: I flow in faith and trust God's perfect timing for my life.

Glow-Up Challenge: Instead of rushing something today, release it and pray, "Lord, make it beautiful in Your time."

Restored to Shine

Day 234
Restored Boundaries

August 22

"Above all else, guard your heart, for everything you do flows from it."
Proverbs 4:23

Restoration often requires protection. Healthy boundaries aren't barriers. They're spiritual borders that keep your peace intact.

Affirmation: I guard my peace with love. Boundaries protect my glow.

Glow-Up Challenge: Identify one boundary you need to strengthen and take one small action to honor it today.

Restored to Shine

Day 235
Overflowing Grace

August 23

"And from His fullness, we all received, Grace upon Grace."
2 Corinthians 9:8

When grace overflows, effort becomes ease. You don't have to strive. You just have to stay surrendered. Restoration means operating from grace, not grind.

Affirmation: I overflow with grace. Everything I need flows freely from God.

Glow-Up Challenge: Give yourself permission to slow down today. Grace, not guilt, is your motivator.

Restored to Shine

Day 236
Restored Mindset

August 24

"Be transformed by the renewing of your mind."
Romans 12:2

Restoration starts in your thoughts. When you align your mindset with God's truth, you see everything through the lens of peace instead of pressure.

Affirmation: My mind is renewed daily. I think with peace, faith, and purpose.

Glow-Up Challenge: Catch one negative thought and replace it with a truth from Scripture.

Restored to Shine

Day 237
The Glow of Generosity

August 25

"God loves a cheerful giver."
2 Corinthians 9:7

Restored hearts love to give, not from obligation, but overflow. Generosity keeps your spirit soft and your blessings in motion.

Affirmation: I give joyfully. Generosity multiplies my light.

Glow-Up Challenge: Surprise someone with kindness today. Give from your overflow.

Restored to Shine

Day 238
Restored Vision

August 26

"For the vision awaits its appointed time... though it linger, wait for it; it will certainly come."
Habakkuk 2:3

Restoration brings clarity, not all at once, but at the right time. Trust that every dream still alive in your heart is unfolding under divine direction.

Affirmation: My vision is clear and divinely guided. God's timing perfects every detail.

Glow-Up Challenge: Revisit a dream you set aside. Pray over it and ask God to renew it with purpose.

Restored to Shine

Day 239
Walking in Wholeness

August 27

"I pray that you may enjoy good health and that all may go well with you, even as your soul is getting along well."
3 John 1:2

Wholeness isn't just about healing. It's about harmony. When body, mind, and spirit walk in unity, your glow shines effortlessly from the inside out.

Affirmation: I walk in wholeness, harmony, and divine health.

Glow-Up Challenge: Do one nourishing thing for your body, one for your mind, and one for your spirit today.

Restored to Shine

Day 240
Freedom in Faith

August 28

"It is for freedom that Christ has set us free."
Galatians 5:1

Restoration brings freedom from fear, shame, and striving. Your responsibilities remain, but the weight lifts. You're free to live fully, love deeply, and shine brightly.

Affirmation: I am free in Christ. I am light, loved, and limitless.

Glow-Up Challenge: Do one thing today that makes you feel free. Dance, worship, breathe, or simply rest in joy.

Restored to Shine

Day 241
Restored Purpose

August 29

"The Lord will fulfill his purpose for me; your steadfast love, O Lord, endures forever."
Psalm 138:8

God doesn't just restore your heart. He restores your why. Your purpose may look new, but it's always been written in His plan.

Affirmation: My purpose is restored and aligned with God's divine blueprint.

Glow-Up Challenge: Reflect on one way God has redirected your purpose for good. Thank Him for the detour.

Restored to Shine

Day 242
Living in Overflow

August 30

"Blessed is she who has believed that the Lord would fulfill His promises to her."
Luke 1:45

Overflow comes when you stop doubting what God already declared. You're walking proof of promise, living in abundance, not anxiety.

Affirmation: I live in overflow. My faith keeps every promise alive.

Glow-Up Challenge: Declare one promise from Scripture out loud today. Believe it's already fulfilled.

Restored to Shine

Day 243
Restored Identity

August 31

"In Him we were also chosen, having been predestined according to the plan of Him who works out everything."
Ephesians 1:11

When you remember who you are in Christ, you stop striving to prove yourself. You don't have to chase identity. It's already secure in divine love.

Affirmation: I am chosen, cherished, and created on purpose for a purpose.

Glow-Up Challenge: Write down five truths about your identity in Christ. Keep them where you can see them daily.

Restored to Shine

Day 244
The Glow of Gratitude Renewed

September 1

"Worship the Lord with gladness; come before Him with joyful songs."
Psalm 100:2

Gratitude is the rhythm of the restored heart. When you wake up thankful, you attract more reasons to stay that way.

⚜

Affirmation: My heart sings with gratitude. Joy is my daily language.

Glow-Up Challenge: Create a short "morning praise list" of three things you'll thank God for before the day begins.

Restored to Shine

Day 245
Strength in Surrender

September 2

"For when I am weak, then I am strong."
2 Corinthians 12:10

Surrender doesn't mean giving up. It means going deeper. True restoration happens when you stop fighting and start flowing with grace.

Affirmation: My surrender strengthens me. I trust God's perfect plan.

Glow-Up Challenge: Identify one area you're still trying to control. Give it back to God in prayer.

Restored to Shine

Day 246
Living Restored

September 3

"Our mouths were filled with laughter, our tongues with songs of joy… The Lord has done great things for us."
Psalm 126:2–3

This is your moment of laughter, joy, and lightness. You've walked the journey. Now live the testimony. Your restoration is real, radiant, and ready to ripple out into the world.

Affirmation: I live restored, radiant with joy, anchored in peace, and overflowing with grace.

Glow-Up Challenge: Celebrate your transformation today. Write or speak aloud: "The Lord has done great things for me!"

Restored to Shine

Day 247
Steady in the Light

September 4

"They will have no fear of bad news; their hearts are steadfast, trusting in the Lord."
Psalm 112:7

When your heart is healed, you no longer panic when life changes. Restoration brings a steady glow. One that's grounded in peace, not circumstance.

Affirmation: My peace is steady. I trust God through every shift and season.

Glow-Up Challenge: When something unexpected arises today, pause and say, "I am steady in the light."

Restored to Shine

Day 248
Restored Rhythm

September 5

"Learn from Me... for My yoke is easy and My burden is light."
Matthew 11:29–30

Restoration creates rhythm. An ease that comes from walking with God instead of rushing ahead of Him. When your soul aligns with His pace, peace flows naturally.

Affirmation: I move in divine rhythm. Peace sets my pace.

Glow-Up Challenge: Slow down one routine task today. Breathe, savor, and do it with presence.

Restored to Shine

Day 249
Flourishing Faith

September 6

"Planted in the house of the Lord, they will flourish in the courts of our God."
Psalm 92:13

You've outgrown survival. Now you're thriving. Flourishing faith means you no longer live in fear of what's next. You're rooted in trust and blooming in every area.

Affirmation: I am flourishing in faith. Growth and grace surround me.

Glow-Up Challenge: Reflect on one area of your life that's flourishing, and thank God for the fruit.

Restored to Shine

Day 250
Restored Voice

September 7

"Let them give glory to the Lord and proclaim His praise in the islands."
Isaiah 42:12

Restoration gives your voice back. The same mouth that once spoke pain now proclaims praise. Your words are power. Use them to glorify and uplift.

Affirmation: My voice carries light. I speak life, not limitation.

Glow-Up Challenge: Share one truth or encouragement today. Online, in person, or in prayer.

Restored to Shine

Day 251
The Glow of Graceful Growth

September 8

"Forgetting what is behind and straining toward what is ahead."
Philippians 3:13–14

Graceful growth means you don't rush the process. You honor it. You've healed enough to move forward without the weight of what once was.

Affirmation: I grow with grace. My past prepared me, but it no longer defines me.

Glow-Up Challenge: Write down one lesson you've learned from your past that's helping you grow today.

Restored to Shine

Day 252
Restored Radiance

September 9

"Then you will look and be radiant, your heart will throb and swell with joy."
Isaiah 60:5

Restoration is visible. Others see it. The peace in your eyes, the joy in your spirit, the light in your presence. You are glowing from the inside out.

Affirmation: My restoration shines through every part of my being.

Glow-Up Challenge: Look in the mirror today and speak this aloud: "This is what restoration looks like."

Restored to Shine

Day 253
Legacy of Light

September 10

"No one lights a lamp and puts it in a place where it will be hidden, or under a bowl. Instead they put it on its stand, so that those who come in may see the light."
Luke 11:33

Your glow-up was never just for you. It's for generations to come. Every prayer, every tear, every healed part of you becomes a legacy of light that keeps shining long after you.

Affirmation: I am leaving a legacy of light and love for those who follow.

Glow-Up Challenge: Write a note, prayer, or message to the next generation. Blessing them to walk in God's light.

Restored to Shine

Day 254
Sustained by Grace

September 11

"My grace is sufficient for you, for My power is made perfect in weakness."
2 Corinthians 12:9

Restoration doesn't mean perfection. It means presence. Grace sustains what strength cannot. When you lean into grace, you stay restored even when life wobbles.

Affirmation: Grace carries me daily. I don't strive, I surrender.

Glow-Up Challenge: When you feel pressure today, pause and say, "Grace is enough for me right now."

Restored to Shine

Day 255
Restored Vision and Focus

September 12

"Where there is no vision, the people perish."
Proverbs 29:18

Restoration renews your heart and sharpens your focus. God brings clarity where there was confusion and vision where there was discouragement.

Affirmation: My vision is clear, my focus is strong, and my eyes stay on God's purpose.

Glow-Up Challenge: Write down your top three priorities for this season, and invite God to be at the center of each.

Restored to Shine

Day 256
Faith-Filled Finishing

September 13

"Let us hold unswervingly to the hope we profess, for He who promised is faithful."
Hebrews 10:23

Restoration includes endurance and finishing what God started in you. Faith-filled finishing means you stay steady until the promise is fulfilled.

Affirmation: I finish with faith, knowing God's promise is still unfolding.

Glow-Up Challenge: Reflect on one goal or prayer still in progress. Thank God for the process, not just the outcome.

Restored to Shine

Day 257
The Glow of Humility

September 14

"Humble yourselves before the Lord, and He will lift you up."
James 4:10

Humility is the hidden beauty of restoration. You shine not because you're elevated, but because you stayed surrendered. The glow of humility is gentle, powerful, and lasting.

Affirmation: I shine through humility. My heart remains soft before God.

Glow-Up Challenge: Compliment or uplift someone else today. Celebrate their light as much as your own.

Restored to Shine

Day 258
Restored Routine

September 15

"Let all things be done decently and in order."
1 Corinthians 14:40

God blesses structure that flows with grace. Restored living means finding rhythm in your daily life. One that nourishes your body, mind, and spirit.

Affirmation: My daily rhythms reflect peace, order, and divine flow.

Glow-Up Challenge: Create one simple morning or evening ritual that helps you feel aligned and calm.

Restored to Shine

Day 259
Restored Connection

September 16

"My command is this: Love each other as I have loved you."
John 15:12

Restoration reconnects you to others through empathy, love, and understanding. God heals isolation by drawing you into divine community.

Affirmation: My relationships are restored through love, empathy, and grace.

Glow-Up Challenge: Reach out to someone you haven't spoken to in a while. Reconnect from a place of love, not obligation.

Restored to Shine

Day 260
Overflowing Light

September 17

"If you spend yourselves in behalf of the hungry... your light will rise in the darkness."
Isaiah 58:10

When you pour from overflow, not emptiness, your glow expands. Giving becomes your greatest joy, and your restoration blesses others effortlessly.

Affirmation: My light overflows. I give from abundance, not depletion.

Glow-Up Challenge: Offer kindness today without expecting anything in return. Let your glow do the giving.

Restored to Shine

Day 261
Peaceful Presence

September 18

"Be still, and know that I am God."
Psalm 46:10

Restoration deepens your presence. No more rushing, just resting in awareness of God's nearness. Peace becomes your posture, not your pursuit.

Affirmation: I move through each moment with calm. I am anchored in God's presence.

Glow-Up Challenge: Spend five minutes today in silence. Just breathing and feeling God's peace surround you.

Restored to Shine

Day 262
Strength in Still Seasons

September 19

"The Lord will fight for you; you need only to be still."
Exodus 14:14

Even in stillness, you are growing. Restoration doesn't require constant motion. It thrives in trust. When you pause, Heaven still moves.

Affirmation: My stillness is strength. God works while I rest.

Glow-Up Challenge: Resist the urge to rush progress. Let one thing unfold naturally today.

Restored to Shine

Day 263
The Glow of Gratitude Everlasting

September 20

"Whatever you do, whether in word or deed, do it all in the name of the Lord Jesus, giving thanks."
Colossians 3:17

Gratitude sustains your glow. It turns every ordinary day into sacred ground and keeps restoration alive in your spirit.

Affirmation: Gratitude fills every breath. My heart overflows with thanksgiving.

Glow-Up Challenge: Write or voice a prayer of thanks tonight. Name specific ways God has blessed your journey.

Restored to Shine

Day 264
Purpose in Peace

September 21

"You will keep in perfect peace those whose minds are steadfast, because they trust in you."
Isaiah 26:3

Your purpose doesn't need pressure. It's revealed in peace. When your spirit is calm, your calling becomes clear.

Affirmation: My peace guides me toward my purpose. I trust the gentle leading of God.

Glow-Up Challenge: Ask yourself, "What brings me peace?" Then take one step closer to that place or practice.

Restored to Shine

Day 265
The Beauty of Balance

September 22

"There is a time for everything, and a season for every activity under the heavens."
Ecclesiastes 3:1

Balance is the quiet strength of restoration. You've learned when to move and when to rest. When to give, and when to simply be.

Affirmation: I live in divine balance. Productive, peaceful, and perfectly paced.

Glow-Up Challenge: Simplify something in your schedule today. Create more room for peace.

Restored to Shine

Day 266
Restored Radiance in Community

September 23

"Let us consider how we may spur one another on toward love and good deeds."
Hebrews 10:24–25

Restoration glows brighter together. When you shine beside others walking in faith, the light multiplies.

Affirmation: I am part of a radiant community of faith and love.

Glow-Up Challenge: Encourage someone today who's on their own healing or faith journey. Be their light.

Restored to Shine

Day 267
The Overflow of Wholeness

September 24

"Now to Him who is able to do immeasurably more than all we ask or imagine."
Ephesians 3:20

This is the promise of restoration. Not just enough, but overflow. Wholeness means you no longer chase. You attract through alignment and grace.

Affirmation: My life overflows with abundance, peace, and divine fulfillment.

Glow-Up Challenge: End your day by saying, "Thank You, Lord. You've done more than I could have imagined."

Restored to Shine

Day 268
Restored Confidence in Calling

September 25

"The One who calls you is faithful, and He will do it."
1 Thessalonians 5:24

You don't have to question your calling. Just keep walking in it. God's faithfulness fulfills what He starts, and your obedience keeps it glowing.

Affirmation: I am confident in my calling. God is completing His work in me.

Glow-Up Challenge: Speak over yourself today: "What God started in me will be finished beautifully."

Restored to Shine

Day 269
The Glow of Contentment

September 26

"I have learned to be content whatever the circumstances."
Philippians 4:11

Contentment is the quiet power of restoration. When you're grateful for what is, you attract what's meant to be.

Affirmation: I am content and complete in every season. Peace fills my present.

Glow-Up Challenge: Spend five minutes today naming what you already have that you once prayed for.

Restored to Shine

Day 270
Restored Hope

September 27

"Everything that was written in the past was to teach us, so that through endurance... we might have hope."
Romans 15:4

Restoration rekindles hope. The steady kind that doesn't fade when life shifts. Hope is faith's flame that keeps your spirit glowing in every season.

Affirmation: Hope rises within me daily. I am anchored in God's promises.

Glow-Up Challenge: Write one hopeful declaration for your future and read it every morning this week.

Restored to Shine

Day 271
Grace for the Journey

September 28

"Grace and peace be yours in abundance through the knowledge of God."
2 Peter 1:2

Grace is the oil that keeps your light burning. You no longer strive to shine. Grace keeps you glowing effortlessly.

Affirmation: I walk in overflowing grace. Peace follows every step I take.

Glow-Up Challenge: Extend grace to yourself today. Forgive one small mistake or release self-pressure.

Restored to Shine

Day 272
Restored Radiance in Purpose

September 29

"Those who are wise will shine like the brightness of the heavens, and those who lead many to righteousness, like the stars for ever and ever."
Daniel 12:3

Your purpose shines brighter now because it's no longer about performance. It's about presence. You glow because you're aligned, not because you're trying.

Affirmation: I radiate divine purpose. My light glorifies God, not me.

Glow-Up Challenge: Do something purposeful today that reflects your faith. Even in a simple act of kindness.

Restored to Shine

Day 273
Living in Overflow

September 30

"You crown the year with Your bounty, and Your carts overflow with abundance."
Psalm 65:11

Restoration means overflow. Blessings spilling from every corner of your life. You're surrounded by evidence of God's goodness.

Affirmation: I am crowned with favor. Abundance flows wherever I go.

Glow-Up Challenge: Write down five ways God has blessed you recently big or small and celebrate each one.

Restored to Shine

Day 274
The Glow of Graceful Living

October 1

"For the grace of God has appeared that offers salvation to all people."
Titus 2:11–12

Graceful living is the final form of restoration. A heart so full of peace that it naturally overflows into everything you do.

Affirmation: My life flows with grace. Calm, kind, and Christ-centered.

Glow-Up Challenge: Be intentional about moving gracefully today. In your tone, pace, and posture.

Restored to Shine

Day 275
Faith That Finishes Well

October 2

"I have fought the good fight, I have finished the race, I have kept the faith."
2 Timothy 4:7

Restoration means running your race with grace. You no longer sprint to prove yourself. You pace yourself with purpose, trusting God's timing for your finish line.

Affirmation: I am finishing well. Strong in faith and grounded in grace.

Glow-Up Challenge: Reflect on one area of life where God helped you persevere. Write a thank-you prayer for the journey.

Restored to Shine

Day 276
Restored in Reflection

October 3

"Search me, God, and know my heart."
Psalm 139:23–24

Reflection is a sacred act of restoration. Pausing to let God show you how far you've come allows you to see what He's still refining. Growth never stops, and neither does grace.

Affirmation: I invite God to search my heart and keep refining me with love.

Glow-Up Challenge: Take a few minutes to journal where you've grown most this year. Emotionally, spiritually, or mentally.

Restored to Shine

Day 277
Steadfast Joy

October 4

"Do not grieve, for the joy of the Lord is your strength."
Nehemiah 8:10

Restored joy isn't fragile. It's fierce. It's not dependent on what happens around you but anchored in Who lives within you.

Affirmation: My joy is strong, steady, and unshakable.

Glow-Up Challenge: Smile intentionally today, even through challenges, and whisper, "My joy is strength."

Restored to Shine

Day 278
Living as Light

October 5

"Let your light so shine before others, that they may see your good works and give glory to your Father in heaven."
Matthew 5:16

You're no longer searching for light. You are it. Radiant restoration means living as a vessel of love, peace, and compassion in every space you enter.

Affirmation: I live as light. Radiating love and grace wherever I go.

Glow-Up Challenge: Walk into every room today knowing your presence brings warmth and calm.

Restored to Shine

Day 279
The Power of Praise

October 6

"Let everything that has breath praise the Lord."
Psalm 150:6

Praise keeps restoration alive. It's the rhythm of a heart that remembers Who healed it. Gratitude turns into worship, and worship keeps your soul glowing.

Affirmation: My praise is my power. Gratitude keeps my glow alive.

Glow-Up Challenge: Turn on a worship song and sing or dance freely. Let joy move through your whole being.

Restored to Shine

Day 280
Restored Radiance Through Service

October 7

"Each of you should use whatever gift you have received to serve others."
1 Peter 4:10

When you serve from overflow, restoration becomes contagious. Your gifts were never meant to stay hidden. They're meant to bless others and magnify God's glory.

Affirmation: I serve from overflow. My gifts are blessings to the world.

Glow-Up Challenge: Use one of your gifts to bless someone today. Freely, joyfully, and without expectation.

Restored to Shine

Day 281
Peace That Prevails

October 8

"For everyone born of God overcomes the world. This is the victory that has overcome the world, even our faith."
1 John 5:4

Restoration doesn't remove challenges. It changes your response to them. You've learned how to glow through storms and stay peaceful in the process.

Affirmation: My peace prevails. I overcome with quiet confidence in God.

Glow-Up Challenge: End your day in gratitude for how far you've come. Say out loud, "I am restored, radiant, and rooted in peace."

Restored to Shine

Day 282
The Glow of Consistency

October 9

"Let us not become weary in doing good, for at the proper time we will reap a harvest if we do not give up."
Galatians 6:9

Consistency is the quiet fuel of restoration. The more faithfully you walk with God, the more naturally your glow shines, steady, strong, and sure.

Affirmation: My consistency in faith keeps my light shining bright.

Glow-Up Challenge: Choose one small daily habit that nurtures your spirit, and commit to it this week.

Restored to Shine

Day 283
Restored Courage

October 10

"Be strong and courageous. Do not be afraid... for the Lord your God goes with you."
Deuteronomy 31:6

Courage after restoration isn't about fighting. It's about following. You move boldly now because you know Who walks before you.

Affirmation: My courage is fueled by faith. I move boldly with divine confidence.

Glow-Up Challenge: Take one brave action today toward something new or unfamiliar.

Restored to Shine

Day 284
The Beauty of Becoming

October 11

"We all… are being transformed into His image with ever-increasing glory."
2 Corinthians 3:18

Restoration isn't a finish line. It's a lifelong transformation. Every day you reflect more of God's light and grow deeper into His likeness.

Affirmation: I am becoming more radiant every day. I am growing in grace and glory.

Glow-Up Challenge: Look back at who you were six months ago. Write down the growth you now see.

Restored to Shine

Day 285
Divine Simplicity

October 12

"What does the Lord require of you? To act justly, love mercy, and walk humbly with your God."
Micah 6:8

A restored life is a simple one. It is filled with love, kindness, and humility. You don't need to complicate what God has already made clear.

Affirmation: I live simply, love deeply, and walk humbly with God.

Glow-Up Challenge: Simplify your day. Remove one unnecessary thing and focus on peace.

Restored to Shine

Day 286
Anchored Assurance

October 13

"We have this hope as an anchor for the soul, firm and secure."
Hebrews 6:19

Assurance is the quiet strength of restoration. When life shifts, your hope stays anchored and steady through the winds of change.

Affirmation: My soul is anchored in unshakable faith and divine assurance.

Glow-Up Challenge: Write down one situation that feels uncertain and declare: "My anchor holds."

Restored to Shine

Day 287
Restored Relationships with God

October 14

"Come near to God and He will come near to you."
James 4:8

Restoration always leads you home, closer to His heart. As you draw near to God, you find that peace, purpose, and power are all byproducts of His presence.

Affirmation: I am close to God. His love restores me daily.

Glow-Up Challenge: Spend 10 minutes in quiet communion. No requests, just connection.

Restored to Shine

Day 288
The Glow of Graceful Endings

October 15

"He who was seated on the throne said, 'I am making everything new!'"
Revelation 21:5

Every ending in God's hands becomes a beginning. Restoration teaches you to release with peace, knowing that every close carries new creation.

Affirmation: I release the old with grace and welcome every new beginning.

Glow-Up Challenge: Reflect on one chapter of your life that ended, and thank God for what it taught you.

Restored to Shine

Day 289
Restored Rhythms of Renewal

October 16

"Because of the Lord's great love we are not consumed... His compassions never fail. They are new every morning."
Lamentations 3:22–23

Restoration is refreshed daily. Every sunrise brings new grace, new mercy, and a fresh chance to glow brighter than yesterday.

Affirmation: Every morning is a new beginning. I rise renewed in grace.

Glow-Up Challenge: Begin your morning with gratitude before reaching for your phone. Thank God for one new mercy today.

Restored to Shine

Day 290
The Glow of Gentle Power

October 17

"She is clothed with strength and dignity; she can laugh at the days to come."
Proverbs 31:25

Restoration gives you a kind of strength that doesn't shout. It shines. Gentle power is the quiet confidence of a heart fully at peace.

Affirmation: My strength is gentle, my spirit is steady, and my confidence is divine.

Glow-Up Challenge: Face one challenge today with calm assurance instead of reaction. Let peace lead your response.

Restored to Shine

Day 291
Restored Radiance in Purpose

October 18

"But he knows the way that I take; when he has tested me, I will come forth as gold."
Job 23:10

Even the detours were divine. Restoration reveals that every twist in your story led you right into purpose.

Affirmation: Everything in my life is working together for divine good.

Glow-Up Challenge: Write a "thank you" note to your past self for surviving, learning, and staying faithful.

Restored to Shine

Day 292
Restored Rest

October 19

*"Come to Me, all you who are weary and burdened,
and I will give you rest."*
Matthew 11:28

Restoration requires rest for body and soul. Rest is not laziness. It's holy alignment with the rhythm of grace.

Affirmation: Rest restores my soul and renews my light.

Glow-Up Challenge: Schedule intentional stillness today. No productivity, just presence.

Restored to Shine

Day 293
The Radiance of Obedience

October 20

"To obey is better than sacrifice."
1 Samuel 15:22

Obedience keeps restoration flowing. When you listen and respond to God's guidance, your path remains illuminated with purpose.

Affirmation: I walk in obedience. My yes to God keeps me glowing in grace.

Glow-Up Challenge: Take one small step of obedience today, even if it feels simple or unseen.

Restored to Shine

Day 294
Restored Wonder

October 21

"Many, Lord my God, are the wonders You have done."
Psalm 40:5

Restoration opens your eyes to wonder again. To notice the divine details in every ordinary moment. Wonder is worship that whispers, "Wow, God, You're still doing miracles."

Affirmation: My heart is full of wonder. I see God's miracles all around me.

Glow-Up Challenge: Pause three times today to notice beauty in nature, people, or simple grace moments.

Restored to Shine

Day 295
Radiant Resilience

October 22

*"We are hard pressed on every side, but not crushed...
struck down, but not destroyed."
2 Corinthians 4:8–9*

Restoration doesn't make you untouchable. It makes you unbreakable. Radiant resilience is the glow that remains after every storm passes.

Affirmation: I am resilient, radiant, and restored. Nothing can dim the light God placed within me.

Glow-Up Challenge: Reflect on one trial that shaped your strength and thank God for the resilience it built.

Restored to Shine

Day 296
The Beauty of Becoming Whole

October 23

"He who began a good work in you will carry it on to completion until the day of Christ Jesus."
Philippians 1:6

Restoration isn't about arrival. It's about continual becoming. God is still perfecting you, polishing every piece until your glow reflects His glory.

Affirmation: I am whole, and yet still becoming all God designed me to be.

Glow-Up Challenge: Write down three ways you've changed this year, and how God's hand shaped each transformation.

Restored to Shine

Day 297
Restored Gratitude

October 24

"Give thanks to the Lord, for He is good; His love endures forever."
Psalm 107:1

Gratitude is the heartbeat of restoration. The more you thank Him, the more your eyes open to the beauty of what already is.

Affirmation: Gratitude magnifies my glow and multiplies my blessings.

Glow-Up Challenge: Speak three "thank yous" to God out loud today: one for your past, one for your present, and one for your future.

Restored to Shine

Day 298
Radiant Wholeness

October 25

"And the peace of God, which transcends all understanding, will guard your hearts and your minds Christ Jesus."
Philippians 4:7

Wholeness feels like peace that doesn't need explanation. When Christ rules your heart, you stop needing control, and start living from calm confidence.

Affirmation: I live in peaceful wholeness. My heart is ruled by divine calm.

Glow-Up Challenge: Spend 10 minutes journaling what "peaceful wholeness" looks like for you emotionally, spiritually, and physically.

Restored to Shine

Day 299
Restored Joy in Simplicity

October 26

"You make known to me the path of life; You will fill me with joy in Your presence."
Psalm 16:11

True joy is found in simplicity. The quiet moments with God that remind you you're already complete. It springs from where you place your heart.

Affirmation: My joy flows from simple, sacred moments with God.

Glow-Up Challenge: Simplify your evening. Light a candle, play soft worship, and just be with Him.

Restored to Shine

Day 300
The Glow of Unwavering Peace

October 27

"You will keep in perfect peace those whose minds are steadfast, because they trust in You."
Isaiah 26:3

Peace is the proof of restoration. It doesn't mean there's no chaos. It means your heart no longer matches it.

Affirmation: My peace is unshakable because my trust is immovable.

Glow-Up Challenge: When stress appears today, pause and breathe out, "Peace still reigns here."

Restored to Shine

Day 301
Restored to Overflow

October 28

"I have come that they may have life, and have it to the full."
John 10:10

Fullness is God's promise. Not survival, but abundance. When you're restored, you no longer live half-lit. You radiate wholeness in every area.

Affirmation: I live fully and freely in the abundance of God's love.

Glow-Up Challenge: Treat yourself to something that celebrates your growth. A walk, a bath, a worship playlist, or simple joy.

Restored to Shine

Day 302
The Radiance of Surrender

October 29

"Commit your way to the Lord; trust in Him and He will do this."
Psalm 37:5

Surrender is the ultimate glow. When you let go, God lifts you higher, and your peace becomes proof that you're held in divine hands.

Affirmation: I trust God completely. My surrender is my strength.

Glow-Up Challenge: Release one lingering worry or goal to God tonight. Visualize laying it at His feet.

Restored to Shine

Day 303
Faith That Keeps Glowing

October 30

"Now faith is confidence in what we hoped for and assurance about what we do not see."
Hebrews 11:1

Restoration strengthens even the smallest faith. It's not about how much faith you have, but how deeply it's rooted in God's power.

Affirmation: My faith shines brighter each day. Small seeds, big miracles.

Glow-Up Challenge: Write down one area of life where you want to see a miracle, and pray over it with mustard-seed faith.

Restored to Shine

Day 304
Restored Radiance in Rest

October 31

*"In peace I will lie down and sleep, for You alone,
Lord, make me dwell in safety."
Psalm 4:8*

Restoration includes sacred rest. When you rest, you trust that God works even when you don't. Sleep becomes worship when it's anchored in peace.

Affirmation: My rest is holy. My peace is protected.

Glow-Up Challenge: Turn off screens early tonight. Go to bed grateful, trusting that God restores you while you rest.

Restored to Shine

Day 305
The Beauty of Still Believing

November 1

"'Everything is possible for one who believes.'"
Mark 9:23

Belief is restoration's constant companion. Even when outcomes shift, belief keeps you glowing. It helps you build faith in God's goodness no matter the season.

Affirmation: I still believe: in God's timing, in His promises, and in my purpose.

Glow-Up Challenge: Speak this aloud three times today: "I still believe, even here."

Restored to Shine

Day 306
Restored Purpose in Presence

November 2

"I keep my eyes always on the Lord. With Him at my right hand, I will not be shaken."
Psalm 16:8

Your presence in this world is purpose fulfilled. You shine not by doing more, but by being fully with Him in every moment.

Affirmation: My purpose is presence. I live intentionally and glow continually.

Glow-Up Challenge: Be fully present in one simple activity today eating, walking, or talking and feel God's nearness in it.

Restored to Shine

Day 307
The Glow of Grateful Obedience

November 3

"If you love Me, keep My commands."
John 14:15

Grateful obedience flows naturally from a restored heart. You no longer obey out of fear, but from fullness. Love that overflows into action.

Affirmation: My obedience is worship. My actions reflect love.

Glow-Up Challenge: Do one thing today purely out of love for God. No pressure, just joy.

Restored to Shine

Day 308
Restored Strength in Stillness

November 4

"In repentance and rest is your salvation, in quietness and trust is your strength."
Isaiah 30:15

Stillness isn't inactivity. It's divine strength. Restoration matures your spirit to know when to rest and when to rise.

❀

Affirmation: My quiet trust is my greatest strength.

Glow-Up Challenge: Take 10 minutes to sit in silence with no agenda. Just breath in peace and exhale worry.

Restored to Shine

Day 309
Fully Restored, Forever Radiant

November 5

"I am the Alpha and the Omega, the Beginning and the End."
Revelation 21:6

Restoration is eternal. It's the continual renewal that flows from a God who never stops making things new. You are fully restored, and your glow is everlasting.

Affirmation: I am forever radiant, made new daily by the One who restores all things.

Glow-Up Challenge: Light a candle tonight as a symbol of your eternal glow. Whisper a prayer of thanks for the journey.

Restored to Shine

Day 310

The Grace of Consistent Peace

November 6

*"Now may the Lord of peace himself give you peace at
all times and in every way."*
2 Thessalonians 3:16

Peace becomes permanent when you allow it to rule, not visit. Restored peace is a steady rhythm. It's what guides every thought, word, and reaction.

Affirmation: Peace reigns within me. I choose calm over chaos every time.

Glow-Up Challenge: Notice what disturbs your peace today, and gently release it through prayer instead of reaction.

Restored to Shine

Day 311
Restored Confidence in God's Plan

November 7

"Commit to the Lord whatever you do, and He will establish your plans."
Proverbs 16:3

Restoration anchors your confidence in the Planner, not the plan. When you commit everything to God, peace replaces pressure.

Affirmation: I trust God's blueprint. Every detail unfolds in divine timing.

Glow-Up Challenge: Surrender one current goal or decision. Whisper, "Lord, make it Yours."

Restored to Shine

Day 312
The Glow of Gratitude in Motion

November 8

"Rejoice always, pray continually, give thanks in all circumstances."
1 Thessalonians 5:16–18

When gratitude moves with you, it becomes your rhythm. A grateful heart keeps your glow in motion even through ordinary days.

Affirmation: Gratitude fuels my glow. I walk with joy in every step.

Glow-Up Challenge: Write a quick gratitude list mid-day. Thank God for five things you might otherwise overlook.

Restored to Shine

Day 313
Restored Vision for the Future

November 9

"Call to Me and I will answer you and tell you great and unsearchable things you do not know."
Jeremiah 33:3

Restoration clears your spiritual sight. You see both your path and your Guide. That vision becomes a partnership with God.

Affirmation: My vision is clear and Spirit-led. I see through the lens of faith.

Glow-Up Challenge: Ask God to show you a glimpse of your next season, then listen for His gentle nudge.

Restored to Shine

Day 314
Radiant Renewal

November 10

"Though outwardly we are wasting away, yet inwardly we are being renewed day by day."
2 Corinthians 4:16

Restoration is an inside job. Even as the world changes, your inner glow renews daily. It's the secret strength that never fades.

Affirmation: I am renewed daily. My spirit glows brighter with every breath of grace.

Glow-Up Challenge: Spend 5 minutes breathing intentionally. Inhale "renewal," exhale "release."

Restored to Shine

Day 315
Restored Reverence

November 11

"The fear of the Lord is the beginning of wisdom."
Psalm 111:10

Reverence is awe that anchors restoration. When you keep your heart in wonder at God's goodness, your life naturally aligns with wisdom.

Affirmation: I live in reverence and awe. Wisdom flows through my worship.

Glow-Up Challenge: Pause and marvel at one detail of God's creation today. The sky, a tree, a person, or a moment of beauty.

Restored to Shine

Day 316
The Glow of Completion

November 12

"The peace of God, which transcends all understanding, will guard your hearts and your minds in Christ Jesus."
Philippians 4:7

Completion in Christ doesn't mean the journey ends. It means you've reached peace. Your glow is now constant, steady, and guarded by His love.

Affirmation: I am complete in Christ. Glowing in peace that surpasses all understanding.

Glow-Up Challenge: Reflect tonight on your growth. Whisper, "Thank You, Lord, for finishing what You started."

Restored to Shine

Day 317
The Glow of Unshakable Trust

November 13

"Trust in the Lord forever, for the Lord, the Lord Himself, is the Rock eternal."
Isaiah 26:4

Restoration builds an unshakable trust. Even when life wavers, your heart stays steady on the Rock. That's the peace of a woman who's found her footing in faith.

Affirmation: My trust is firm and fearless. I am anchored in the eternal Rock.

Glow-Up Challenge: When uncertainty arises, place your hand over your heart and say, "I am safe in His strength."

Restored to Shine

Day 318
Restored Harmony Within

November 14

"May the words of my mouth and the meditation of my heart be pleasing in Your sight."
Psalm 19:14

True restoration aligns your thoughts, words, and spirit with divine peace. Harmony within creates healing without.

Affirmation: My heart, mind, and spirit live in divine harmony.

Glow-Up Challenge: Speak only words of grace today. If it doesn't bring peace, let silence speak for you.

Restored to Shine

Day 319
Faith That Flourishes in Stillness

November 15

"My Presence will go with you, and I will give you rest."
Exodus 33:14

Flourishing faith doesn't need noise to grow. It blooms quietly in the soil of stillness where God's presence waters the roots.

Affirmation: I flourish in stillness. God's presence nourishes my soul.

Glow-Up Challenge: Spend time today in quiet reflection. No asking, just receiving His peace.

Restored to Shine

Day 320
The Radiance of Restoration

November 16

"The Lord will guide you always... you will be like a well-watered garden."
Isaiah 58:11

You are the living image of restoration. You are nourished, grounded, and glowing with divine life. Your peace waters others simply by existing.

Affirmation: I am a well-watered garden. Flourishing in God's care.

Glow-Up Challenge: Do one thing that refreshes your soul today. A walk, worship, or laughter with a friend.

Restored to Shine

Day 321
Restored Hope for Tomorrow

November 17

"For I know the plans I have for you… plans to give you a hope and a future."
Jeremiah 29:11

Restored hope allows you to look ahead without fear. You don't need to know the future. You trust the One who's already there.

Affirmation: My future is secure in God. My hope shines brighter each day.

Glow-Up Challenge: Write a note to your future self. Speak blessings and faith over the woman you're becoming.

Restored to Shine

Day 322
Grace That Keeps Glowing

November 18

"And God is able to bless you abundantly... so that you will abound in every good work."
2 Corinthians 9:8

Grace never runs out. It regenerates. The more you pour out love, the more grace refills your glow. Restoration flows endlessly from divine supply.

Affirmation: I am continually refilled by grace. My glow never dims.

Glow-Up Challenge: Do one generous act today. Give joyfully, knowing grace replenishes what you release.

Restored to Shine

Day 323
Restored Identity in Christ

November 19

"You also, like living stones, are being built into a spiritual house to be a holy priesthood."
1 Peter 2:5

Restoration reveals your royal identity. You no longer wonder who you are. You walk boldly as God's beloved, shining from a place of worth.

Affirmation: I am chosen, royal, and radiant. My identity is rooted in Christ.

Glow-Up Challenge: Stand tall today. Remind yourself, "I am God's masterpiece, walking in light."

Restored to Shine

Day 324
The Strength of Serenity

November 20

"God is within her, she will not fall; God will help her at break of day."
Psalm 46:5

Restoration brings serenity that feels like strength. A quiet confidence that comes from knowing God is within you, not just around you.

Affirmation: I am calm, grounded, and held. Serenity is my strength.

Glow-Up Challenge: Begin your morning with three slow breaths and say, "God is within me; I will not fall."

Restored to Shine

Day 325
Restored Joy That Multiplies

November 21

"Now is your time of grief, but I will see you again and you will rejoice, and no one will take away your joy."
John 16:22

Restored joy can't be stolen. It's anchored in eternity, not emotion. The kind of joy you carry now is proof of Heaven's touch on your heart.

Affirmation: My joy is divine, lasting, and untouchable.

Glow-Up Challenge: Do something today that reignites childlike joy. Laugh freely, sing loudly, or dance without reason.

Restored to Shine

Day 326
The Glow of Grace in Action

November 22

"Let your conversation be always full of grace, seasoned with salt."
Colossians 4:6

Grace in action is restoration in motion. Kindness that lingers, gentleness that heals, and love that leaves a mark.

※

Affirmation: I speak with grace, move with love, and leave light wherever I go.

Glow-Up Challenge: Offer encouraging words to someone today. Remind them of their light.

Restored to Shine

Day 327
Restored Balance

November 23

"The one who fears God will avoid all extremes."
Ecclesiastes 7:18

Balance is sacred. It's knowing when to pour and when to pause, when to speak and when to simply be still. Restoration brings rhythm, not rush.

Affirmation: I live balanced, grounded, and guided by divine wisdom.

Glow-Up Challenge: Protect your peace by saying "no" to one unnecessary thing today, and "yes" to rest.

Restored to Shine

Day 328
Faith That Flourishes Forever

November 24

"I am like an olive tree flourishing in the house of God; I trust in God's unfailing love forever and ever."
Psalm 52:8

Flourishing faith is rooted and renewable. It never stops growing because it's planted in eternal love.

Affirmation: My faith flourishes forever. It is rooted in unfailing love.

Glow-Up Challenge: Reflect on one way your faith has grown this year, and give thanks for the fruit it's bearing.

Restored to Shine

Day 329
The Radiance of Gratitude

November 25

"Praise the Lord, my soul, and forget not all His benefits."
Psalm 103:2

Gratitude keeps your light pure. The more you remember His goodness, the brighter your radiance becomes.

Affirmation: Gratitude keeps my glow alive. I remember and rejoice in His goodness.

Glow-Up Challenge: Write a gratitude list focused only on spiritual blessings such as peace, healing, forgiveness, love.

Restored to Shine

Day 330
Restored for Eternity

November 26

"So we fix our eyes not on what is seen, but on what is unseen... what is unseen is eternal."
2 Corinthians 4:18

Restoration doesn't end with this life. It continues eternally. Every healed part of you reflects Heaven's work, preparing you for glory beyond measure.

Affirmation: My restoration is eternal. I live with Heaven's glow within.

Glow-Up Challenge: End your night in stillness. Whisper a prayer of thanks for the eternal restoration already at work in you.

Restored to Shine

Day 331
The Glow of Holy Confidence

November 27

"The Lord is my light and my salvation, whom shall I fear?"
Psalm 27:1

Holy confidence isn't arrogance. It's assurance. You no longer question your worth or your calling, because you know Who walks with you.

Affirmation: My confidence is holy. I walk boldly in God's light.

Glow-Up Challenge: Stand in front of a mirror and say aloud, "I am chosen, called, and covered."

Restored to Shine

Day 332
Restored Restfulness

November 28

"There remains, then, a Sabbath-rest for the people of God."
Hebrews 4:9–10

Restoration invites rest, not just physically but spiritually. A calm knowing that everything is already handled in Heaven's time.

Affirmation: I rest in divine timing. My peace is my proof of faith.

Glow-Up Challenge: Unplug from all screens or noise for 30 minutes. Let your soul breathe in sacred quiet.

Restored to Shine

Day 333
The Beauty of Blessing Others

November 29

"A generous person will prosper; whoever refreshes others will be refreshed."
Proverbs 11:25

The restored soul becomes a blessing to others, giving love, grace, and light freely because her source is endless.

Affirmation: My life blesses others. I give freely from divine overflow.

Glow-Up Challenge: Find one way to refresh someone else today through encouragement, prayer, or kindness.

Restored to Shine

Day 334
Restored Depth

November 30

"I pray that you… may have power to grasp how wide and long and high and deep is the love of Christ."
Ephesians 3:17–19

The deeper your roots reach in love, the stronger your glow. Restoration isn't shallow. It's soul-deep, reaching every corner of your being.

Affirmation: I am rooted in love, restored in depth, and grounded in grace.

Glow-Up Challenge: Spend five quiet minutes reflecting on how deeply loved you truly are.

Restored to Shine

Day 335
The Glow of Overflowing Faith

December 1

"Praise be to the God and Father of our Lord Jesus Christ! In his great mercy he has given us new birth into a living hope through the resurrection of Jesus Christ from the dead."
1 Peter 1:3

Your faith now overflows. Joy and peace are no longer occasional. They are your natural state. You radiate assurance in every season.

Affirmation: My faith overflows with joy, peace, and radiant hope.

Glow-Up Challenge: Speak one positive declaration of faith out loud every hour today. Even simple phrases like "God's got this."

Restored to Shine

Day 336
Restored Purpose Through Peace

December 2

"The fruit of that righteousness will be peace; its effect will be quietness and confidence forever."
Isaiah 32:17

Peace produces the kind of purpose that doesn't demand attention but makes quiet impact. You are living proof that peace and power can coexist.

Affirmation: My purpose flows from peace. I lead with quiet confidence.

Glow-Up Challenge: Do one task today slowly and mindfully. Let peace guide your every move.

Restored to Shine

Day 337
Fully Restored, Eternally Shining

December 3

"They will not need the light of a lamp or the light of the sun, for the Lord God will give them light."
Revelation 22:5

This is the essence of restoration: becoming so filled with God's light that you no longer depend on external sources. His glow is your forever illumination.

Affirmation: God's light shines through me now and for eternity.

Glow-Up Challenge: Light a candle tonight and pray: "Lord, may my light always reflect Yours."

Restored to Shine

Day 338
The Glow of Content Peace

December 4

"I have learned the secret of being content... I can do all things through Christ who strengthens me."
Philippians 4:12–13

Contentment is restoration's final lesson. When your peace is no longer conditional, you've reached the heart of wholeness.

Affirmation: My peace is complete. I am content in every season.

Glow-Up Challenge: Each time you feel lack today, breathe and whisper, "I already have everything I need in Him."

Restored to Shine

Day 339
Restored Joy in Service

December 5

"As we have opportunity, let us do good to all people."
Galatians 6:10

Restoration naturally pours out as service. Your healed heart seeks to bless, not from duty, but from delight.

Affirmation: I serve with joy. My giving glorifies God.

Glow-Up Challenge: Look for a quiet way to serve today: a prayer, a favor, a word of love.

Restored to Shine

Day 340
The Beauty of Enduring Faith

December 6

"Let us fix our eyes on Jesus, the author and perfecter of our faith."
Hebrews 12:2

Enduring faith keeps your glow steady, even when seasons shift. Restoration isn't a destination. It's a lifelong gaze fixed on grace.

Affirmation: My faith endures. My eyes remain on Jesus.

Glow-Up Challenge: Reflect on one time you stayed faithful through difficulty. Thank God for the endurance He built in you.

Restored to Shine

Day 341
Restored Radiance in Relationships

December 7

"Bear with each other and forgive one another... And over all these virtues put on love."
Colossians 3:13–14

Love is the crown of restoration. It's what ties every healing together and lets your light heal others without words.

Affirmation: Love covers all I do. My relationships glow with grace.

Glow-Up Challenge: Reach out to someone you've drifted from. Extend kindness or forgiveness.

Restored to Shine

Day 342
The Glow of Overflowing Gratitude

December 8

"Give thanks to the Lord, for He is good. His love endures forever."
Psalm 136:1

Gratitude keeps the heart freshly restored. The more you thank Him, the more you see His hand in every detail.

Affirmation: Gratitude keeps my glow alive. I overflow with thanksgiving.

Glow-Up Challenge: Write a short "gratitude prayer". Name everything beautiful God has done this year.

Restored to Shine

Day 343
Restored Strength in Still Waters

December 9

"He refreshes the weary and satisfies the faint."
Jeremiah 31:25

You've learned to walk with calm confidence, not rushing, not resisting. Just flowing in His peace. This is the rhythm of the restored.

Affirmation: I walk beside still waters. My soul stays refreshed.

Glow-Up Challenge: Spend 10 minutes outdoors or near water today. Breathe deeply and feel His restoration wash over you.

Restored to Shine

Day 344
Fully Restored, Glowing with Grace

December 10

"Be of one mind, live in peace. And the God of love and peace will be with you."
2 Corinthians 13:11

This is the posture of restoration. Living in peace, guided by love, and glowing with divine harmony. You no longer seek balance. You are balance.

Affirmation: I am fully restored. Glowing in grace, guided by peace, and anchored in love.

Glow-Up Challenge: End your night in prayerful gratitude. Thanking God for bringing you into wholeness and light.

Restored to Shine

Day 345
The Glow of Abiding Peace

December 11

"Remain in Me, as I also remain in you. No branch can bear fruit by itself."
John 15:4

Abiding peace is the reward of restoration and a calm assurance that you and God are inseparable. You no longer chase peace. You live in it.

Affirmation: I abide in divine peace. Rooted, rested, and radiant.

Glow-Up Challenge: Take 10 minutes of silence today to simply abide. No requests, just presence with God.

Restored to Shine

Day 346
Restored Joy That Shines Outward

December 12

"This is the day the Lord has made; let us rejoice and be glad in it."
Psalm 118:24

Restoration makes your joy contagious. When you rejoice, your glow reaches others, lighting hearts that need to remember joy is still possible.

Affirmation: My joy shines beyond me. I am a reflection of Heaven's happiness.

Glow-Up Challenge: Smile intentionally at three people today. Let your light speak louder than words.

Restored to Shine

Day 347
The Strength of a Restored Heart

December 13

"A cheerful heart is good medicine."
Proverbs 17:22

A restored heart is unburdened, light, and healed from within. Your glow now comes from joy that flows freely. It is medicine for you and everyone around you.

Affirmation: My heart is healed and strong. Joy is my daily medicine.

Glow-Up Challenge: Do something today that makes your heart genuinely happy. No guilt, just joy.

Restored to Shine

Day 348
Restored Faith in Every Season

December 14

"He has made everything beautiful in its time."
Ecclesiastes 3:11

Faith after restoration trusts every season, even the quiet ones. You no longer fear the waiting. You see the beauty in the becoming.

Affirmation: Every season holds beauty. My faith grows through them all.

Glow-Up Challenge: Reflect on one past season that shaped your strength and thank God for its lessons.

Restored to Shine

Day 349
The Glow of Overflowing Love

December 15

"Dear friends, let us love one another, for love comes from God."
1 John 4:7

Love is the purest glow of all. Restored hearts radiate compassion because they've been touched by unconditional grace.

Affirmation: My life is love in motion. It is gentle, generous, and grace-filled.

Glow-Up Challenge: Express love intentionally today through kind words, a note, or a simple act of care.

Restored to Shine

Day 350
Restored Vision Through Gratitude

December 16

"Your word is a lamp for my feet, a light on my path."
Psalm 119:105

Gratitude sharpens your spiritual sight. When you thank God for where you are, your path ahead glows clearer than ever.

Affirmation: Gratitude lights my path. I see every step through grace.

Glow-Up Challenge: Journal one page of gratitude for the past year. Big moments and quiet miracles alike.

Restored to Shine

Day 351
The Radiance of a Renewed Spirit

December 17

"Create in me a clean heart, O God, and renew a right spirit within me."
Psalm 51:10

Even restoration needs refreshing, a daily renewal of your spirit that keeps your glow alive and pure.

Affirmation: My spirit is renewed daily. My glow never fades, it flourishes.

Glow-Up Challenge: End your day with worship. Praise Him for restoring you and keeping you bright.

Restored to Shine

Day 352
Restored Faith That Flows

December 18

"Be still before the Lord and wait patiently for Him."
Psalm 37:7

Your faith flows easily now. It requires no forcing, no fearing, just trusting. Restoration turns your waiting into worship and your silence into peace.

Affirmation: I am patient and peaceful. My faith flows freely in God's timing.

Glow-Up Challenge: Take five quiet minutes today to simply breathe and repeat: "I trust Your timing, Lord."

Restored to Shine

Day 353
The Glow of Unfailing Grace

December 19

"My grace is sufficient for you, for My power is made perfect in weakness."
2 Corinthians 12:9

Grace never runs dry. Restoration teaches you that God's love fills every gap, every flaw, every fragile place, and makes it shine.

Affirmation: Grace fills me, fuels me, and keeps me glowing through everything.

Glow-Up Challenge: Instead of criticizing yourself today, respond to every imperfection with grace.

Restored to Shine

Day 354
Restored Courage to Continue

December 20

"Be strong and courageous... for the Lord your God will be with you wherever you go."
Joshua 1:9

Courage after restoration looks different. It is softer, wiser, and deeply rooted. You're not fearless. You're faith-full.

Affirmation: I move forward with holy courage. God walks with me into every tomorrow.

Glow-Up Challenge: Take one bold step toward a dream you've delayed. No matter how small, just start.

Restored to Shine

Day 355
The Beauty of Divine Balance

December 21

"A false balance is abomination to the Lord, but a just weight is His delight."
Proverbs 11:1

Balance is the heartbeat of restoration. You're finding rhythm and peace in motion. You've learned when to pour, when to pause, and how to glow in both.

Affirmation: I live in divine balance. My rest and my work both glorify God.

Glow-Up Challenge: Create space in your schedule today for both stillness and joy.

Restored to Shine

Day 356
The Glow of Ongoing Renewal

December 22

"Who satisfies your desires with good things so that your youth is renewed like the eagle's."
Psalm 103:5

Restoration is not a moment. It's maintenance. Renewal is the daily act of aligning your thoughts with truth and your spirit with grace.

Affirmation: I am renewed daily in peace, purpose, and divine perspective.

Glow-Up Challenge: Replace one recurring negative thought with a Scripture-based truth today.

Restored to Shine

Day 357
Restored through Reflection

December 23

"I remember the days of long ago; I meditate on all Your works and consider what Your hands have done."
Psalm 143:5

Reflection refreshes your faith. Looking back reminds you just how faithful God has been, and how far He's carried you.

Affirmation: I reflect with gratitude. My past proves God's power and grace.

Glow-Up Challenge: Write a short "praise timeline" of your year. Include the big and small ways God has shown up.

Restored to Shine

Day 358
Radiant Beyond Measure

December 24

"For you were once darkness, but now you are light in the Lord. Live as children of light for the fruit of the light consists in all goodness, righteousness and truth."
Ephesians 5:8-9

This is your divine glow realized. A radiant spirit reflecting the One who restores you. You are light in motion, love in bloom.

Affirmation: I shine effortlessly for God's glory. My life is His radiant reflection.

Glow-Up Challenge: End your day by lighting a candle and praying, "May my light draw others to You."

Restored to Shine

Day 359
The Glow of Grateful Completion

December 25

"I thank my God every time I remember you."
Philippians 1:3

Today, as the world pauses to celebrate the birth of Christ, your heart pauses to give thanks for all He has birthed within you. This year was a journey of healing and becoming. Every prayer, every tear, every moment of faith has led you to a place of holy gratitude and radiant peace.

Affirmation: I celebrate the birth of new beginnings within me and give thanks for every grace along the way.

Glow-Up Challenge: Take a quiet moment by the light of your tree or candle and whisper a prayer of thanksgiving, for Jesus, for this journey, and for the glow that now lives within you.

Restored to Shine

Day 360
Restored Purpose, Renewed Vision

December 26

"Write the vision; make it plain."
Habakkuk 2:2

You've healed, grown, and glowed. Now it's time to dream again. Restoration renews your purpose and expands your vision beyond what you imagined.

Affirmation: My purpose is clear and Spirit-led. I see through eyes of faith.

Glow-Up Challenge: Write three Spirit-inspired goals or dreams for your next season.

Restored to Shine

Day 361
The Beauty of Eternal Joy

December 27

"Weeping may last for a night, but joy comes in the morning."
Psalm 30:5

Your mornings are now filled with joy that never fades. Every tear became a seed for the harvest of happiness you now live in.

❦

Affirmation: My joy is eternal. Every sorrow has turned into song.

Glow-Up Challenge: Share your joy. Tell someone how God turned one of your darkest moments into light.

Restored to Shine

Day 362
Restored Faith, Renewed Fire

December 28

"Fan into flame the gift of God."
2 Timothy 1:6

Restoration reignites the fire within you through renewed passion for your calling. Your glow deepening.

Affirmation: My faith is on fire. My glow ignites others to believe.

Glow-Up Challenge: Pray for renewed boldness. Ask God to rekindle every gift He's placed inside you.

Restored to Shine

Day 363
The Glow of Graceful Transition

December 29

"See, I am doing a new thing!"
Isaiah 43:19

Even endings are beginnings in disguise. God is already writing your next chapter, glowing with promise and peace.

Affirmation: I embrace new beginnings with peace and expectation.

Glow-Up Challenge: Reflect on what you're releasing and what you're ready to receive next.

Restored to Shine

Day 364
Fully Restored, Perfectly Whole

December 30

"May God Himself... sanctify you through and through."
1 Thessalonians 5:23

You are whole. Body, mind, and spirit. Restoration has reached every layer of your being, and your life now sings of sacred renewal.

Affirmation: I am whole, healed, and holy. My restoration glorifies God.

Glow-Up Challenge: Write down three words that describe who you've become through this journey.

Restored to Shine

Day 365
Shine from Within

December 31

"You are the light of the world."
Matthew 5:14

This is your holy glow-up realized. You've journeyed from roots to radiance, from healing to wholeness. Your light is no longer borrowed. It's birthed. Keep shining, keep believing, keep glowing from within.

Affirmation: I am restored to shine. Radiant, rooted, and redeemed.

Glow-Up Challenge: Celebrate this moment. Light a candle, worship, and declare: "This light is mine, and it's here to stay."

Closing Reflection
Fully Restored & Radiantly Alive

Take a deep breath, beloved.
You made it.

You've walked through valleys, climbed mountains, and let your heart be refined by God's light. What began as a search for healing has become a lifestyle of holiness: and wholeness. Every prayer, every verse, every tear, and triumph along the way has shaped you into the radiant vessel you are today.

Your roots grew deep in Christ.

Your heart was healed from within.
Your spirit learned to glow through the storm.
Your faith became radiant.
And now, you are restored to shine.

You no longer chase light. You carry it.
You no longer look for peace. You live it.
You no longer wait for renewal. You walk in it.

This is what divine restoration looks like: showing up fully and surrendering completely.

Your glow is Spirit-given.
As you step forward into new seasons, remember: Every time you choose peace over pressure, you're glowing. Every time you speak love instead of fear, you're glowing.
Every time you trust God in uncertainty, you're glowing.

You are proof that healing happens.
You are evidence that faith still works.
You are light, and the world needs your glow.

Final Blessing

Holy Glow, Holy Flow

May your heart remain open to divine renewal.
May your peace be unshakable and your faith ever-bright.
May you walk in grace that overflows and love that transforms.
May your roots stay deep, your spirit stay lifted, and your glow never fade.

When you look back, may you see not what broke you, but what built you. When you look ahead, may you move with the confidence of one who knows she's covered and when you stand still, may you feel Heaven smiling, because you've become a reflection of its light.

Keep glowing, beautiful soul.
Keep rising, keep trusting, keep shining from within.
You are restored to shine, today, tomorrow, and forever

Author's Note
From My Heart to Yours

Dear Beautiful Soul,

If you are reading this, it means you've walked this journey: one day, one prayer, one glow at a time. And from the deepest part of my heart, I want to say thank you.

When God placed the vision for Holy Glow-Up in my spirit, I had no idea it would become such a sacred path of transformation. Each page was birthed from seasons of surrender, healing, and restoration in my own life. I didn't write these devotionals for you as much as I wrote them with you as a sister who knows what it feels like to be broken, rebuilt, and reborn in Christ's light.

Through every verse, reflection, and affirmation, my prayer has been that you wouldn't just read about the glow: but that you'd feel it stirring within you. I pray that this book would remind you that healing is holy, that your journey matters, and that your light is needed in this world.

May you always remember: you are rooted in grace, healed by love, and restored by divine design. You are not behind, you are becoming. And even when the world feels dim, the light within you will never go out, because it's lit by the One who never fades.

Thank you for walking this path with me, for glowing beside me, for believing again, and for reminding me that God truly makes all things new.

Keep shining, beautiful friend.
You are, and always will be, His masterpiece in motion.

With love and light,
Kelley McConnell
Crossroad to Healing
Rooted in Christ. Guided in Healing. Restored to Shine

A Note from Kelley:

If this devotional has touched your heart, helped you rediscover your light, or brought you closer to God's presence, I would love to hear from you. Your reflections, testimonies, and reviews help this message reach more women and girls who are ready to shine from within.

If you feel led, please take a moment to leave a short review on Amazon, it means more than you know.

And if you'd like to share your Holy Glow-Up journey on Instagram, tag @crossroadtohealing, @HolyGlowUp365 or use the hashtag #HolyGlowUp so we can celebrate your light together.

With gratitude and radiant love,

Kelley

About the Author
Kelley McConnell

Kelley McConnell is the founder of Crossroad to Healing, a Christ-centered wellness ministry dedicated to helping others restore body, mind, and spirit through faith, holistic healing, and divine balance.

A visionary practitioner, mentor, and author, Kelley is also the creator of the IASIS Healing Method: a Christ-centered, Spirit-led healing approach that helps individuals experience deep restoration and alignment with God's design for wholeness. Through IASIS and her RESTORE Nutritional Healing program, she has guided countless souls toward renewed peace, purpose, and spiritual vitality.

Kelley's heart beats for women who are ready to rise: to release what's heavy, reclaim their joy, and glow in the fullness of who God created them to be. Her writing blends warmth, wisdom, and worship, inspiring others to live whole, holy, and fully lit by His love.

When she's not creating, teaching, or writing, you'll find her grounding in nature, spending time with her family, or sharing her light through everyday acts of kindness. She believes that the truest form of beauty is a peaceful heart, and that every woman carries a divine glow waiting to be revealed.

Holy Glow-Up: 365 Days to Shine from Within is Kelley's devotional debut: a heartfelt offering of faith and restoration, written to remind every reader that no matter where she stands, her glow still lives within.

www.ingramcontent.com/pod-product-compliance
Lightning Source LLC
Chambersburg PA
CBHW020217170426
43201CB00007B/241